K7 C0-BQC-966

ALL LIFE IS
PROBLEM SOLVING

ALL LIFE IS
PROBLEM SOLVING

Karl Popper

Translated by Patrick Camiller

London and New York

CB
357
.P5613
1999

First published 1999
by Routledge
11 New Fetter Lane, London EC4P 4EE

Simultaneously published in the USA and Canada
by Routledge
29 West 35th Street, New York, NY 10001

First published in German 1994 by Piper Verlag, Munich
Alles Leben ist Problemlösen © 1994 Karl Popper
This edition © 1999 the Estate of Karl Popper
Translation © 1999 Routledge

The right of Karl Popper to be identified as the Author of this
Work has been asserted by him in accordance with the Copyright,
Designs and Patents Act 1988

Typeset in Garamond by
M Rules
Printed and bound in Great Britain by
MPG Books Ltd, Bodmin

All rights reserved. No part of this book may be reprinted or
reproduced or utilized in any form or by any electronic,
mechanical, or other means, now known or hereafter
invented, including photocopying and recording, or in any
information storage or retrieval system, without permission in
writing from the publishers.

British Library Cataloguing in Publication Data
A catalogue record for this book is available from the British Library

Library of Congress Cataloging in Publication Data
Popper, Karl Raimund, Sir
[Alles Leben ist Problemlösen. English]
All life is problem solving / Karl R. Popper
'This collection of essays and talks may be seen as a sequel to In Search of a
Better World' – Pref.
1. Civilization, Modern – Philosophy. 2. Science – Philosophy.
3. Science – History. I. Title.
CB357.P5613 1999
192–dc21 98-46132

ISBN 0 415 17486 4

CONTENTS

CONTENTS

PUBLISHER'S NOTE

In this translation, four chapters have been omitted from the original German version of *Alles Leben ist Problemlösen*, since all have appeared previously in English, in either identical or slightly varied form, in other works of the author published by Routledge: Chapter 2, 'Wissenschaftliche Reduktion und die essentielle Unvollständigkeit der Wissenschaft', is Addendum 2 of *The Open Universe. An Argument for Indeterminism*, 1982; Chapter 8, 'Über Geschichtsschreibung und über den Sinn der Geschichte', forms the bulk of Chapter 25 of *The Open Society and Its Enemies*, 1945 (5th edition, 1966); and Chapter 10, 'Bemerkungen zur Theorie und Praxis des demokratischen Staates' and Chapter 11, 'Freiheit und intellektuelle Verantwortung', are Chapters 8 and 9 respectively of *The Lesson of This Century*, 1997.

The omitted chapters have been replaced by 'Towards an evolutionary theory of knowledge' (Chapter 5), 'Masaryk and the open society' (Chapter 14), and 'How I became a philosopher without trying' (Chapter 15). All were originally written in English.

'The collapse of communism' (Chapter 12) was also written in English and translated into German for *Alles Leben ist Problemlösen*. This volume publishes the English original for the first time.

The translation from German was made by Patrick Camiller, and revised by Melitta Mew and David Miller, to echo Karl Popper's English style as closely as possible.

PREFACE

This collection of essays and talks may be seen as a sequel to my book *In Search of a Better World*. Both contain some contributions strongly oriented towards the natural sciences, and others strongly oriented towards history or politics. The title *All Life is Problem Solving* is also the title of Chapter 9, which strongly influenced the short but relevant 'Summary By Way of a Preface' in that earlier collection. Here too, I have tried to give the preface more weight than prefaces usually have.

The selection of chapters has been made with the help and advice of my assistant, Mrs Melitta Mew, and Dr Klaus Stadler from Piper Verlag. I am deeply grateful to them both.

I

The first part of this book is called 'Questions of natural science'. What I have in mind are mainly biology and the unfathomable wealth of living forms.

The more deeply we penetrate into the many areas of biology, from whichever angle, the more unfathomable does the wealth of biological structures prove to be, and the more prodigious their harmonious interplay.

The last chapter in Part I is devoted to Johannes Kepler, the great seeker after harmonies in God's physical creation, and the great discoverer of the three laws that determine the motion of the planets in a highly abstract yet highly harmonious manner. Of the three intellectual giants who together, and with others, created our natural science – the contemporaries Galileo and Kepler, and their successor Newton – Kepler is perhaps the greatest. His is certainly the most attractive, open, and modest personality. All three were passionate seekers and tireless workers; all three toiled extremely hard, often with persistently disappointing results, but they were amply rewarded with the great joy of those who see the world in a new light – differently, more beautifully and harmoniously, and also better than anyone before them – and who then know that their hard work has been crowned with joy, almost undeserved because it could so easily have turned out otherwise.

Of the three great figures, Kepler was the only one who not only worked everything out but honestly and conscientiously wrote it all down. He also understood, as no one else did, that it was the Greek thinkers of the distant past – from Thales to Aristotle, Aristarchus, and Ptolemy – who had bequeathed their boldest ideas to Kepler's inspirational model, Copernicus.

More than in the other two cases, it was his great modesty that again and again helped Kepler to see and learn from his own mistakes – mistakes that could be overcome only with the utmost difficulty. Each of the three intellectual giants was, in his own way, caught up in a superstition. ('Superstition' is a word we should use only with the greatest caution, knowing how little we know and how certain it is that we too, without realizing it, are caught up in various forms of superstition.) Galileo most deeply believed in a natural circular motion – the very belief that Kepler, after lengthy struggles, conquered both in himself and in astronomy. Newton wrote a long book on the traditional (mainly biblical) history of mankind, whose dates he adjusted in accordance with principles quite clearly derived from superstition. And Kepler was not only an astronomer but also an astrologer; he was for this reason dismissed by Galileo and many others.

But Kepler fought against dogmatic forms of his own astrological superstition: he was a self-critical astrologer. He taught that the fate written in the stars was not inexorable but could be mastered by our moral will. It was a major concession to the critics of astrology. Of the three great men, he was perhaps the least dogmatic in his superstition.

II

The second part of this book, 'Thoughts on history and politics', consists of a number of occasional pieces. It offers no advice or prescriptions, least of all infallible ones, but it does make the case for an attitude of responsibility.

I am naturally in favour of democracy – but not in the way that most of its advocates are. Winston Churchill once said: 'Democracy is the worst form of government, only excepting all other forms of government.' We have nothing better than to abide by majority decisions. A majority government is *accountable*, a coalition government much less so, and a minority government still less.

'Democracy' in the sense of 'rule by the people' has practically never existed, and when it has, it has been an arbitrary and unaccountable dictatorship. A government can and should be accountable to the people. Rule by the people cannot be; it is unaccountable.

I am therefore in favour of *democratically elected, constitutional government*, which is quite different from rule by the people. And I am in favour of accountable government – accountable first of all to those who elected it, but also, perhaps still more, morally responsible to humanity.

Never before have there been so many and such dreadful weapons in so many irresponsible hands – a thousand times more than after the two world wars. The fact that this is so and that our political leaders accept it, is something for which they are accountable to us. We must hold them all to blame for it.

Most of our political leaders would be glad to change how things are. But they have inherited from their predecessors a world situation that was constantly deteriorating because of the gang-leaders' arms race; and they seem, however reluctantly, to have come to terms with it. Any interference seems too risky and difficult. So they talk about it as little as possible.

After the wars there was talk – of disarmament. The Western democracies did disarm to quite a considerable degree. But only they did. This was the great idea of the League of Nations and later, after the Second World War, of the United Nations – the idea that the moral and military superiority of these bodies put them under an obligation to keep the peace, until the others had seen and learnt their duty.

No one can doubt that we are on the point of retreating from this position. We do not explain this to the voters: we are afraid of making sacrifices for it. We prefer not to get involved in 'adventures', a word we use to describe our duty.

III

When I try to think about our European and American history, I come to a conclusion rather like that of the historian H.A.L. Fisher, which I have several times quoted before: 'The fact of progress is written plain and large on the page of history; but progress is not a law of nature. The ground gained by one generation may be lost by the next.'

I can and must agree with each of these three statements. But what is the 'progress' of which Fisher rightly says that history informs us, but which is insecure and capable of being lost?

The answer to this question is as clear as it is important. The progress that Fisher has in mind, that we all have in mind, is ethical or moral progress. It is directed towards the peace on earth already promised in the New Testament, when violence of any kind disappears in both the internal and external relations of states. It is progress towards a civilized human society, progress towards the rule of law and a league of all states based upon the rule of law, with the aim of maintaining peace.

This – according to Kant – is our moral duty: the duty of all men of good will; the goal that we must set for history. Since nuclear weapons appeared, it has been a *necessary* goal.

Not only does this goal have good prospects (as the civilized states are at present also the more powerful); it is necessary. The existence of nuclear weapons makes it a necessary goal for everyone willing to stand up for the progress of humanity and civilization. For the only alternative is annihilation.

The goal originally comes from the Augustan age of the Roman Empire and from the New Testament: *Et in terra pax hominibus bonae voluntatis* ('And peace on earth to all men of good will' – or, as it might also be translated, 'And peace on earth to be gained by all men of good will').

From the crime of the First World War (which led to the Kellogg Pact) and from the crime of the Second World War (which led to the United Nations), a sufficiently strong political movement has arisen among all men of good will.

But, as Fisher says, 'the ground gained by one generation may be lost by the next'.

It has been lost. We have to win it back. We must give thought to our duty. And we must remind our politicians that their responsibility does not end with their death (or resignation).

K.R.P.
Kenley, 12 July 1994

Part I

QUESTIONS OF NATURAL SCIENCE

1

THE LOGIC AND EVOLUTION OF SCIENTIFIC THEORY*

The central idea I should like to present in this talk may be expressed in the following way.

The natural as well as the social sciences always start from *problems*, from the fact that something inspires *amazement* in us, as the Greek philosophers used to say. To solve these problems, the sciences use fundamentally the same method that common sense employs, the method of *trial and error*. To be more precise, it is the method of *trying out* solutions to our problem and then discarding the false ones as erroneous. This method assumes that we work with a large number of *experimental* solutions. One solution after another is put to the test and eliminated.

At bottom, this procedure seems to be the only logical one. It is also the procedure that a lower organism, even a single-cell amoeba, uses when trying to solve a problem. In this case we speak of testing movements through which the organism tries to rid itself of a troublesome problem. Higher organisms are able to *learn* through trial and error how a certain problem should be solved. We may say that they too make testing movements – mental testings – and that to learn is essentially to try out one testing movement after another until one is found that solves the problem. We might compare the animal's successful solution to an *expectation* and hence to a *hypothesis* or a *theory*. For the animal's behaviour shows us that it expects (perhaps unconsciously or dispositionally) that in a similar case the same testing movements will again solve the problem in question.

The behaviour of animals, and of plants too, shows that organisms are geared to laws or regularities. They *expect* laws or regularities in

* A talk given on North German Radio (NDR), 7 March 1972.

3

their surroundings, and I conjecture that most of these expectations are genetically determined – which is to say that they are innate.

A *problem* arises for the animal if an expectation proves to have been wrong. This then leads to testing movements, to attempts to replace the wrong expectation with a new one.

If a higher organism is too often disappointed in its expectations, it caves in. It cannot solve the problem; it perishes.

I would like to present what I have said so far about learning through trial and error in a three-stage model. The model has the following three stages:

1   *the problem;*
2   *the attempted solutions;*
3   *the elimination.*

So, the first stage in our model is *the problem.* The problem arises when some kind of disturbance takes place – a disturbance either of innate expectations or of expectations that have been discovered or learnt through trial and error.

The second stage in our model consists of *attempted solutions* – that is, attempts *to solve the problem.*

The third stage in our model is the *elimination* of unsuccessful solutions.

Pluralism is essential to this three-stage model. The first stage, the problem itself, may appear in the singular; but not the second stage, which I have called 'attempted solutions' in the plural. Already in the case of animals we speak of testing movements, in the plural. There would be little sense in calling one particular movement a testing movement.

Stage 2, the attempted solutions, are thus testing movements and therefore in the plural; they are subject to the *process of elimination* in the third stage of our model.

Stage 3, the *elimination*, is *negative.* The elimination is fundamentally the elimination of *mistakes.* If an unsuccessful or misguided solution is eliminated, the problem remains unsolved and gives rise to new attempted solutions.

But what happens if an attempted solution is eventually successful? Two things happen. First, the successful solution is *learnt.* Among animals this usually means that, when a similar problem appears again, the earlier testing movements, including unsuccessful ones, are briefly and sketchily repeated in their original order; they are run through until the successful solution is reached.

Learning means that unsuccessful or discarded solutions drop more and more to the level of passing references, so that eventually the successful attempt at a solution appears to be almost the only one left. This is the elimination procedure, which depends upon a pluralism of attempted solutions.

The organism may be said to have thus learnt a new *expectation*. We may describe its behaviour by saying that it expects the problem to be solved through testing movements and, in the end, through the final testing movement that is not eliminated.

As we shall soon see, the development of this expectation by the organism has its scientific counterpart in the formation of hypotheses or theories. But before I turn to the formation of scientific theories, I should like to point out another biological application of my three-stage model. My *three-stage model*,

1   *the problem;*
2   *the attempted solutions;*
3   *the elimination,*

may also be understood as the schema of Darwin's theory of evolution. It is applicable not only to the evolution of the individual organism but also to *the evolution of species*. In the language of our three-stage model, a change in either the environmental conditions or the inner structure of the organism produces a *problem*. It is *a problem of species adaptation*: that is, the species can survive only if it solves the problem through a change in its genetic structure. How does this happen in the Darwinian view of things? Our genetic apparatus is such that changes or mutations occur again and again in the genetic structure. Darwinism assumes that, in the terms of our model, these mutations function as Stage 2 *attempted solutions*. Most mutations are fatal: they are deadly for the bearer of the mutation, for the organism in which they occur. But in this way they are *eliminated*, in accordance with Stage 3 of our model. In our three-stage model, then, we must again stress the essential pluralism of the second stage of *attempted solutions*. If there were not *very many* mutations, they would not be worth considering as attempted solutions. We must assume that sufficient *mutability* is essential to the functioning of our genetic apparatus.

Now I can finally turn to my main theme, the theory or logic of science.

My first thesis here is that science is a biological phenomenon. Science has arisen out of prescientific knowledge; it is a quite remarkable continuation of commonsense knowledge, which may in turn be seen as a continuation of animal knowledge.

My second thesis is that our three-stage model is also *applicable to science*.

I mentioned at the outset that, as the Greek philosophers already saw, science starts from *problems*, from *amazement* about something that may be quite ordinary in itself but becomes a problem or a source of amazement for scientific thinkers. My thesis is that each new development in science can be understood only in this way, that its starting point is a *problem* or a *problem situation* (which means the appearance of a problem in a certain state of our accumulated knowledge).

This point is extremely important. The old theory of science taught, and still teaches, that the starting point for science is our sense perception or sensory observation. This sounds at first thoroughly reasonable and persuasive, but it is fundamentally wrong. One can easily show this by stating the thesis: *without a problem, no observation*. If I asked you: 'Please, observe!', then linguistic usage would require you to answer by asking me: 'Yes, but what? *What* am I supposed to observe?' In other words, you ask me to set you a *problem* that can be solved through your observation; and if I do not give you a *problem* but only an *object*, that is already something but it is by no means enough. For instance, if I say to you: 'Please look at your watch', you will still not know what I actually want to have observed. But things are different once I set you the most trivial *problem*. Perhaps you will not be interested in the problem, but at least you will know what you are supposed to find out through your perception or observation. (As an example, you might take the problem of whether the moon is waxing or waning, or which town the book you are reading was published in.)

Why did the old theory wrongly think that in science we start from sense perceptions or observations, and not from problems?

In this respect, the old theory of science was dependent upon the commonsense conception of knowledge. This tells us that our knowledge of the external world is entirely derived from our sense impressions.

I generally have a lot of respect for common sense. I even think that, if we are just a little critical, common sense is the most valuable and reliable counsellor in every possible problem situation. But it is *not always reliable*. And in matters of scientific or epistemological theory, it is extremely important to have a really critical attitude to it.

It is obviously true that our sense organs inform us about the world around us and that they are indispensable for that purpose. But from this we cannot conclude that our knowledge begins with sense perception. On the contrary: our senses, from the point of view of evolutionary theory, are tools that have been formed to solve certain biological *problems*. Apparently, animal and human eyes developed so that living things that are able to change their position and move about may be warned in sufficient time of dangerous encounters with hard objects from which they might receive an injury. From the point of view of evolutionary theory, our sense organs are the outcome of a series of problems and attempted solutions, just as our microscopes or binoculars are. And this shows that, biologically speaking, the problem comes *before* the observation or sense perception: observations or sense perceptions are important aids to our *attempted solutions* and play the main role in their *elimination*. My three-stage model is thus applicable in the following way to the logic or methodology of science.

1   The starting point is always a *problem* or a problem situation.
2   *Attempted solutions* then follow. These always consist of theories, and these theories, being *trials*, are very often wrong: they are and always will be hypotheses or conjectures.
3   In science, too, we learn by *eliminating* our mistakes, by *eliminating* our false theories.

Our three-stage model,

1   *problem;*
2   *attempted solutions;*
3   *elimination,*

may therefore be applied in describing science. This brings us to our central question:

What is distinctive about human science? What is the key difference between an amoeba and a great scientist such as Newton or Einstein?

The answer to this question is that the distinctive feature of science is conscious application of the *critical method*; in Stage 3 of our model, the stage of error elimination, we act in a consciously critical manner.

The critical method alone explains the extraordinarily rapid growth of the scientific form of knowledge, the extraordinary progress of science.

All prescientific knowledge, whether animal or human, is *dogmatic*; and science begins with the invention of the non-dogmatic, critical method.

At any event, the invention of the critical method presupposes a descriptive human *language* in which critical *arguments* can take shape.

Possibly it presupposes even writing. For the essence of the critical method is that our attempted solutions, our theories, and our hypotheses, can be formulated and objectively *presented* in language, so that they become *objects of consciously critical investigation.*

It is very important to appreciate the huge difference between a thought that is only subjectively or privately thought or held to be true, which is a dispositional psychological structure, and the *same* thought when formulated in speech (perhaps also in writing) and thus presented for public discussion.

My thesis is that the step from my unspoken thought: 'It will rain today' to the same spoken proposition 'It will rain today' is a hugely important step, a step over an abyss, so to speak. At first this step, the expression of a thought, does not seem so great at all. But to formulate something in speech means that what used to be part of my personality, my expectations and perhaps fears, is now objectively to hand and therefore available for general critical discussion. The difference is also huge for me personally. The proposition – the prediction, for example – detaches itself from me when it is formulated in speech. It becomes independent of my moods, hopes, and fears. It is *objectified*. It can be *experimentally* endorsed by others as well as by myself, but it can also be *experimentally* disputed. The pros and cons can be weighed and discussed. People can take sides for and against the prediction.

We come here to an important distinction between two meanings of the word *knowledge* [*Wissen*] – *knowledge in the subjective and in the objective sense*. Usually knowledge is thought of as a subjective or mental state. Starting from the verb form 'I know', one explains knowing as a certain kind of belief – that is, a kind of belief that rests upon *sufficient reasons*. This subjective interpretation of the word 'knowledge' has had too strong an influence on the old theory of science. In fact, it is completely useless for a theory of science, because scientific knowledge consists of objective propositions formulated in speech, of hypotheses and problems, not of subjective expectations or convictions.

Science is a product of the human mind, but this product is as objective as a cathedral. When it is said that a proposition is a thought expressed in speech, this is true enough but it does not focus sharply enough on its objectivity. This is connected with an ambiguity of the word 'thought'. As the philosophers Bernard Bolzano and (following him) Gottlob Frege have particularly emphasized, we must distinguish the *subjective thought process* from the *objective content* or the *logical* or *informational* content of a thought. If I say: 'Mohammed's thoughts are very different from Buddha's', I am speaking not of the two men's thought processes but of the logical content of the two doctrines or theories.

Thought processes may stand in causal relationships. If I say: 'Spinoza's theory was *influenced* by Descartes's theory', I am describing a causal relation between two people and stating something about Spinoza's thought processes.

But if I say: 'Spinoza's theory nevertheless contradicts Descartes's on several important points', I am speaking of the objective logical content of the two theories and not about thought processes. The logical content of statements is what I have in mind above anything else when I stress the objective character of human speech. And when I said earlier that only thoughts spoken aloud can be subjected to criticism, I meant that only the logical content of a proposition, not the psychological thought process, can be critically discussed.

I should now like to recall my three-stage model:

1 *problem;*
2 *attempted solutions;*
3 *elimination,*

and my remark that this schema of how new knowledge is acquired is applicable all the way from the amoeba to Einstein.

What is the difference? This question is decisive for the theory of science.

The crucial difference appears in Stage 3, in the *elimination* of attempted solutions.

In the prescientific development of knowledge, *elimination* is something that happens to us: the environment eliminates our attempted solutions; we are not active in the elimination but only passively involved; we *suffer* the elimination, and if it too often destroys our attempted solutions, or if it destroys an attempted solution that was previously successful, it thereby destroys not only the attempted solution but also ourselves as its bearers. This is clear in the case of Darwinian selection.

The crucial novelty of the scientific method and approach is simply that we are actively interested and involved in elimination. The attempted solutions are objectified; we are no longer personally identified with our attempted solutions. However much we may or may not be aware of the three-stage model, the novelty in the scientific approach is that we actively seek to eliminate our attempted solutions. We subject them to criticism, and this criticism operates with every means that we have at our disposal and are able to produce. For example, instead of waiting until our environment refutes a theory or an attempted solution, we try to modify the environment in such a way that it is *as unfavourable as possible* to our attempted solution. We thus put our theories to the test – indeed, we try to put them to the severest test. We do everything to eliminate our theories, for we ourselves should like to discover those theories that are *false*.

The question of how the amoeba differs crucially from Einstein may thus be answered as follows.

The amoeba shuns falsification: its expectation is part of itself, and prescientific bearers of an expectation or a hypothesis are often destroyed by refutation of the expectation or the hypothesis. Einstein, however, made his hypothesis objective. The hypothesis is something outside him, and the scientist can destroy his hypothesis through criticism without perishing along with it. In science we get our hypotheses to die for us.

I have now reached my own hypothesis, the theory that so many supporters of the traditional theory of science have branded as paradoxical. My main thesis is that what distinguishes the scientific approach and method from the prescientific approach is the method of *attempted falsification*. Every attempted solution, every theory, is tested as rigorously as it is possible for us to test it. But a rigorous examination is always an attempt to discover the *weaknesses* in what is being examined. Our testing of theories is also an attempt to detect their weaknesses. The testing of a theory is thus an attempt to refute or to *falsify* the theory.

This does not mean, of course, that a scientist is always happy to falsify one of his own theories. He put the theory forward as an *attempted solution*, and this means that it was meant to stand up to rigorous testing. Many scientists who manage to falsify a promising solution feel personally very disappointed.

Often the aim of falsifying the theory will not be the scientist's personal goal, and quite often a genuine scientist will try to defend against falsification a theory in which he invested great hopes.

This is thoroughly desirable from the point of view of scientific theory; for how else could we distinguish *genuine* falsifications from *illusory* ones? In science we need to form parties, as it were, for and against any theory that is being subjected to serious scrutiny. For we need to have a rational scientific *discussion*, and discussion does not always lead to a clear-cut resolution.

At any event, the *critical* approach is the crucial novelty that makes science what it is, achieved above all through objective, public, linguistic formulation of its theories. This usually leads to a taking of sides and hence to critical discussion. Often the debate is not resolved for many years, as in the case of the famous debate between Albert Einstein and Niels Bohr. Besides, we have no guarantee that every scientific discussion can be resolved. There is nothing that can guarantee scientific progress.

My main thesis, then, is that the novelty of science and scientific method, which distinguishes it from the prescientific approach, is its consciously critical attitude to attempted solutions; it takes an active part in attempts at elimination, in attempts to criticize and falsify.

Conversely, attempts to save a theory from falsification also have their methodological function, as we have already seen. But my thesis is that such a dogmatic attitude is essentially characteristic of *prescientific* thinking, whereas the critical approach involving conscious attempts at falsification leads to *science* and governs *scientific method*.

Although the taking of sides undoubtedly has a function in scientific method, it is in my view important that the individual researcher should be aware of the underlying significance of attempts at falsification and of sometimes successful falsification. For the scientific method is not *cumulative* (as Bacon of Verulam and Sir James Jeans taught); it is fundamentally *revolutionary*. Scientific progress essentially consists in the replacement of earlier theories by later theories. These new theories must be capable of solving all the problems that the old theories solved, and of solving them at least as well. Thus Einstein's theory solves the problem of planetary motion and macro-mechanics in general, at least as well as, and *perhaps better than*, Newton's theory does. But the revolutionary theory starts from new assumptions, and in its conclusions it goes beyond and directly contradicts the old theory. This contradiction allows it to devise experiments that can distinguish the old from the new theory, but only in the sense that they can falsify at least one of the two theories. In fact, the experiments may prove the superiority of the surviving theory, but not its truth; and the surviving theory may soon be overtaken in its turn.

Once a scientist has grasped that this is how things stand, he will himself adopt a critical attitude to his own pet theory. He will prefer to test it himself and even to falsify it, rather than leave this to his critics.

One example, of which I am proud, is my old friend the brain scientist and Nobel prizewinner Sir John Eccles. I first met John Eccles when I gave a series of lectures at the University of Otago in Dunedin, New Zealand. For years he had already been experimentally tackling the problem of how the nerve impulse is conveyed through 'synaptic transmission' from one nerve cell to another. A school working mainly in Cambridge around Sir Henry Dale conjectured that molecules of a chemical 'transmitter substance' cross the synapse (which separates nerve cells) and thus convey the stimulus from one cell to another. Eccles's experiments had shown, however, that the transmission took an extremely short time – too short in his view for the transmitter substance – and he therefore developed a theory of purely electrical transmission of both nerve stimuli and nerve inhibitions.

But I may let Eccles speak for himself:

> Until 1945 I held the following conventional ideas about scientific research – first, that hypotheses grow out of the careful and methodical collection of experimental data. This is the inductive idea of science deriving from Bacon and Mill. Most scientists and philosophers still believe that this is the scientific method. Second, that the excellence of a scientist is judged by the reliability of his developed hypotheses, which, no doubt, would need elaboration as more data accumulate, but which, it is hoped, will stand as a firm and secure foundation for further conceptual development. A scientist prefers to talk about the experimental data and to regard the hypothesis just as a kind of working construct. Finally, and this is the important point: it is in the highest degree regrettable and a sign of failure if a scientist espouses an hypothesis which is falsified by new data so that it has to be scrapped altogether.
>
> That was my trouble. I had long espoused an hypothesis which I came to realize was likely to have to be scrapped, and I was extremely depressed about it. I had been involved in a controversy about synapses [. . .], believing in those days that the synaptic transmission between nerve cells was largely electrical. I admitted that there was a late, slow chemical component, but I believed that the fast transmission across the synapse was electrical.
>
> At that time I learnt from Popper that it was not scientifically disgraceful to have one's hypothesis falsified. That was the best news I had had for a long time. I was persuaded by Popper, in fact, to formulate my electrical hypotheses of excitatory and inhibitory synaptic transmission so precisely and rigorously that they invited falsification – and, in fact, that is what happened to them a few years later, very largely by my

colleagues and myself, when in 1951 we started to do intra-cellular recording from motoneurones. Thanks to my tutelage by Popper, I was able to accept joyfully this death of the brain-child which I had nurtured for nearly two decades and was immediately able to contribute as much as I could to the chemical transmission story which was the Dale and Loewi brain-child.

I had experienced at last the great liberating power of Popper's teachings on scientific method.

There is a strange sequel. It turned out that I had been too precipitate in my complete rejection of the electrical hypotheses of synaptic transmission. The many types of synapse I had worked on were certainly chemical, but now many electrical synapses are known, and in my book on the synapse [Eccles, 1964][1] there are two chapters on electrical transmission, both excitatory and inhibitory!'[2]

It is worth noting that both Eccles and Dale got it wrong with their pathbreaking theories in neurological research; for both thought that their theories were valid for all synapses. Dale's theory was valid for the synapses on which both were working at the time, but it was no more generally applicable than Eccles's theory. Dale's supporters appear never to have recognized this; they were too sure of their victory over Eccles to realize that both sides were guilty of the same (alleged) sin: namely, 'overhasty generalization without waiting for all the relevant data' (which is, however, never practicable).

Elsewhere, in his Nobel Prize biography, Eccles writes: 'Now I can even rejoice in the falsification of a hypothesis I have cherished as my brain-child, for such falsification is a scientific success.'

This last point is extremely important. We are always learning a whole host of things through falsification. We learn not only *that* a theory is wrong; we learn *why* it is wrong. Above all else, we gain a *new and more sharply focused problem*; and a new problem, as we already know, is the real starting point for a new development in science.

You will perhaps have been surprised that I have so often mentioned my three-stage model. I have done this partly to prepare you for a very similar four-stage model, which is typical of science and the dynamics of scientific development. The four-stage model may be derived from our three-stage model (problem, attempted solutions, elimination), because what we do is call the first stage 'the old problem' and the fourth stage 'the new problems'. If we further replace 'attempted solutions' with 'tentative theories', and 'elimination' with 'attempted elimination through critical discussion', we arrive at the four-stage model characteristic of scientific theory.

So it looks like this:

1   *the old problem;*
2   *formation of tentative theories;*
3   *attempts at elimination* through critical discussion, including experimental testing;
4   *the new problems* that arise from the critical discussion of our theories.

My four-stage model allows a whole series of scientific points to be made.

On the problem. Prescientific and scientific problems are initially practical in nature, but with the four-stage cycle they are soon at least partially replaced by theoretical problems. This means that most new problems arise out of the *criticism of theories*: they are internal to theory. This is already true of the problems in Hesiod's cosmogony, and still more of the problems of the Greek pre-Socratic philosophers; and it is true of most problems in the modern natural sciences. The problems are themselves products of theories, and of the difficulties that critical discussion uncovers in theories. These theoretical problems are fundamentally questions regarding *explanations* or explanatory theories: the tentative answers provided by the theories are in fact *attempted explanations.*

Among practical problems we may include the problems of predicting something. But from the *intellectual* standpoint of *pure science* predictions belong to Stage 3 – to the stage of *critical discussion and examination.* They are intellectually interesting because they allow us, in practice and in the real world, to check the validity of our theories or attempted explanations.

We can also see from our four-stage model that we start in science in the middle of a *cycle* of old problems and end with new problems that function in turn as the starting point for a new *cycle.* Because of the cyclical or periodic character of our model we can start at *any* of the four stages. We can begin with *theories*, at Stage 2 of our model. That is, we can say that the scientist starts from an *old theory* and, by critically discussing and eliminating it, arrives at problems that he then tries to solve through *new theories.* Precisely because of the cyclical character, this interpretation is perfectly satisfactory.

Also in its favour is the fact that we may describe the *creation of satisfactory theories* as the *goal* of science. On the other hand, the question of the circumstances in which a theory may be deemed *satisfactory* leads straight back to the *problem as starting point*. For evidently the first demand we make of a theory is that it should *solve* problems in need of explanation, by clearing up the difficulties that constitute the problem.

Finally, we may choose as our starting point the elimination or eradication of theories that have existed up to now. For science may be said always to start from the collapse of a theory. This collapse, this elimination, leads to the problem of replacing the eliminated theory with a better theory.

I personally prefer the *problem* as the starting point, but I am well aware that the *cyclical character of the model* makes it possible to regard any of the stages as the starting point for a new development.

A crucial feature of the new four-stage model is its dynamic character. Each of the stages contains, as it were, an inner logical motivation to go on to the next stage. Science, as it appears in this logical sketch, is a phenomenon to be understood as perpetually *growing*; it is essentially *dynamic*, never something *finished*; there is no point at which it reaches its goal once and for all.

There is also another reason why I prefer the *problem* as starting point. The *distance* between an *old problem* and its successor, the *new problem*, seems to me to be a much more impressive feature of scientific progress than is the distance between old theories and the next generation of new theories that replace the old.

Let us take as an example the Newtonian and Einsteinian theories of gravitation. The distance between the two theories is great, yet it is possible to translate Newtonian theory into Einsteinian language, into the formalism of the so-called tensor calculus. And if one does this – as Professor Peter Havas has done, for example – one finds that the difference between the two theories is merely in the finite speed of gravitational propagation, and thus the finite speed of light c. This means that Havas has succeeded in formulating the Einsteinian theory in such a way that, by replacing the *finite* speed c of gravitational propagation with an *infinite* speed, it becomes identical with the Newtonian theory.

It would be quite misleading to conclude that the whole progress made by the theory lies in the finite speed of gravitational propagation.

I would argue that the progressive and dynamic character of the advance is much clearer if one compares the *problems* discovered by critics of Newtonian theory (Ernst Mach, for instance) with the *problems* discovered by critics of Einsteinian theory (mainly Einstein himself).

Thus, if one compares the old with the new problems, one sees the great distance, the great advance. In effect, only one of the old problems has remained unsolved, the explanation of the so-called Mach principle. This is the requirement that we conceive the *inertia* of heavy masses as an effect of remote cosmic masses. Einstein was very disappointed that his theory did not completely explain this. In fact, his theory of gravity made inertia a result of gravitation; yet if we do away with masses in Einstein's theory of gravity, it collapses into the special theory of relativity, and inertia remains even without being caused by masses.

Einstein himself saw this as one of the main defects of his theory. And the problem of integrating the Mach principle into the theory of gravity has occupied every scientist in this field for half a century.

For reasons such as these, it seems to me better to begin our four-stage model with the *problem*. Anyway the model shows what is new in the dynamic development of science compared with *pre*scientific development – namely, our active involvement in the processes of elimination, through the invention of language, writing, and critical discussion. My main thesis is that science emerged through the invention of critical discussion.

An important conclusion from my main thesis refers to the question of how empirical scientific theories differ from other theories. This is itself not an *empirical* scientific problem but a *theoretical* scientific problem; it is a problem that belongs to the logic or philosophy of science. The answer, which can be derived from my main thesis, is as follows.

An empirical scientific theory differs from other theories because it may be undone by possible experimental results: that is to say, possible experimental results can be described that would falsify the theory if we were actually to obtain them.

I have called the problem of distinguishing empirical scientific theories from other theories the 'demarcation problem' and my proposed solution the 'criterion of demarcation'.

My proposed solution to the demarcation problem is thus the following criterion of demarcation. A theory is part of empirical science if and only if it conflicts with possible experiences and is therefore in principle falsifiable by experience.

I have called this criterion of demarcation the 'falsifiability criterion'.

The falsifiability criterion may be illustrated by many theories.

16

For example, the theory that vaccination protects against smallpox is falsifiable: if someone who has really been vaccinated still gets smallpox, the theory is falsified.

This example may also be used to show that the falsifiability criterion has problems of its own. If one out of a million vaccinated people gets smallpox, we will hardly consider our theory to be falsified. Rather, we will assume that something was wrong with the vaccination or with the vaccine material. And in principle such an escape route is always possible. When we are faced with a falsification, we can always talk our way out somehow or other; we can introduce an auxiliary hypothesis and reject the falsification. We can 'immunize' our theories against all possible falsification (to use an expression of Professor Hans Albert's).

It is not always simple, then, to apply the falsifiability criterion. Yet the falsifiability criterion does have its value. It is applicable to the theory of smallpox vaccination even if the application is not always quite so simple. If the proportion of vaccinated people who get smallpox is roughly the same as (or perhaps even greater than) the proportion of unvaccinated people who get smallpox, then all scientists will give up the theory of vaccine protection.

Let us compare this case with that of a theory that in my view is not falsifiable: Freud's theory of psychoanalysis, for instance. Evidently, this theory could in principle be tested only if we could describe some human behaviour that conflicted with the theory. There are such falsifiable theories of behaviour: for example, the theory that a man who has lived a long time and always been honest will not suddenly, if his financial circumstances are secure, become a thief in his old age.

This theory is certainly falsifiable, and I suspect that here and there falsifying instances do occur, so that the theory is simply *false* in the formulation just given.

But in contrast to this theory, there seems to be no conceivable human behaviour that could refute psychoanalysis. If a man saves another's life by risking his own, or if he threatens the life of an old friend – whatever unusual human behaviour we might imagine – it will not be in contradiction with psychoanalysis. In principle, psychoanalysis can always explain the most peculiar human behaviour. It is therefore not empirically falsifiable; it is not testable.

I am not saying that Freud did not have many correct insights. I am arguing that his theory is not empirical science, that it is strictly untestable.

This contrasts with theories such as our vaccination example, but above all with theories in physics, chemistry, and biology.

Since Einstein's theory of gravitation, we have reasons to suppose that Newtonian mechanics is false, even though it is an excellent approximation. Anyway both Newton's and Einstein's theories are falsifiable, although of course it is always possible to talk one's way out of falsification by means of an immunization strategy. Whereas no conceivable human behaviour would contradict Freud's psychoanalysis, a table's behaviour would contradict Newton's theory if it were to start moving around. If the full tea-cup on my table were suddenly to start dancing, to spin, and to turn, it would be a falsification of Newton's theory – especially if the tea did not spill as a result of all the spinning and turning. One may say that mechanics stands in contradiction to a whole host of imaginable behaviour on the part of physical bodies – quite unlike psychoanalysis, which stands in contradiction to no conceivable human behaviour.

Einstein's theory of gravitation would itself be affected by almost any imaginable violation of Newtonian mechanics, precisely because Newtonian mechanics is such a good approximation to Einsteinian mechanics. In addition, however, Einstein looked particularly for cases that, if observed, would refute *his* theory but not Newton's.

Einstein wrote, for example, that if his predicted redshift in the spectrum of the satellites of Sirius and other white dwarfs had not been found, he would have considered his theory as refuted.

It is interesting, moreover, that Einstein himself had an extremely critical attitude to his own theory of gravitation. Although none of the experimental tests (all proposed by himself) proved unfavourable to his theory, he regarded it as not fully satisfactory on theoretical grounds. He was perfectly well aware that his theory, like all theories in natural science, was a *provisional attempt at a solution* and therefore had a *hypothetical* character. But he went into greater detail than that. He gave *reasons* why his own theory should be seen as incomplete, and as inadequate for his own research programme. And he listed a set of requirements that an adequate theory would have to fulfil.

But what he claimed for his original theory of gravitation was that it represented a *better approximation* to the sought-after theory than did Newton's theory of gravitation, and therefore *a better approximation to the truth*.

The idea of *approximation to the truth* is, in my view, one of the most important ideas in the theory of science. It is bound up with the fact that, as we have seen, critical discussion of competing theories is so important in science. But critical discussion is regulated by certain values. It needs a regulative principle or, in Kantian terminology, a regulative idea.

Among the regulative ideas that govern the critical discussion of competing theories, three are of the greatest significance: first, the idea of *truth*; second, the idea of the logical and empirical *content* of a theory; and third, the idea of a theory's *truth content* and of its *approximation to the truth*.

That the idea of *truth* governs critical discussion can be seen from the fact that we critically discuss a theory in the hope of eliminating *false* theories. This shows that we are guided by the idea of looking for *true* theories.

The second regulative idea – the idea of the *content* of a theory – teaches us to look for theories with a high informative content. Tautologies or trivial arithmetical propositions such as $12 \times 12 = 144$ are devoid of content: they do not solve any empirical-scientific problem. Difficult problems can be solved only by theories with a high logical and empirical content.

The size of that content is what may be described as the *boldness* of a theory. The more we assert with a theory, the greater is the risk that the theory will be *false*. So we do seek the truth, but we are interested only in bold, risky truths. Examples of bold theories with a high logical content are once again Newton's and Einstein's theories of gravitation, the quantum theory of atoms, and the theory of the genetic code, which partly solves the problem of heredity.

Bold theories such as these have a high content – that is, a high logical and a high empirical content.

These two concepts of content may be explained as follows. The logical content of a theory is the *class of its consequences*, that is, the set or class of all propositions that can be *logically derived* from the theory in question – which will be the higher, the greater the number of consequences.

Even more interesting, perhaps, is the idea of the *empirical content* of a theory. To understand this idea, let us start from the fact that an *empirical* natural law or an *empirical* theory *rules out* certain observable occurrences. (The theory 'All ravens are black' rules out the existence of white ravens; and observation of a white raven refutes the theory.) But as we have seen, Freudian psychoanalysis does not rule out any observable occurrences. Its logical content is certainly high, but its empirical content is nil.

The empirical content of a theory may thus be described as the set or class of empirical propositions excluded by the theory – which means, however, the set or class of empirical propositions that contradict the theory.

Let us take a very simple illustration. The theory that *there are no white ravens* contradicts the statement 'Here is a white raven'. It *rules out*, so to speak, the existence of white ravens. The theory that *all ravens are black* has a far greater empirical content. It rules out not only white ravens but also blue, green, and red ravens: the class of excluded propositions is far greater.

An empirical or observational statement that contradicts a theory may be described as a *possible falsification* or a *potential falsifier* of the theory in question. If a possible falsification is actually observed, then the theory is *empirically falsified*.

The statement 'Here is a white raven' is thus a possible falsification both of the low-content theory that there are no white ravens, and of the high-content theory that all ravens are black.

The statement 'On 10 February 1972 a green raven was delivered to the Zoological Gardens in Hamburg' is a possible falsification or a potential falsifier of the theory that all ravens are black, but also of the theory that all ravens are red or blue. If such a statement, such a potential falsifier, is accepted as true on the basis of observation, then all the theories of which it is a falsifier should be regarded as actually falsified. The interesting thing is that the theory says all the more, the greater the number of its potential falsifiers. It says more, and can clear up more problems. Its *explanatory potential* or its *potential explanatory power* is greater.

From this standpoint, we may once again compare Newton's and Einstein's theories of gravitation. What we find is that the empirical content and the potential explanatory power of Einstein's theory are much greater than those of Newton's. For it asserts much more. It describes not only all kinds of motion that Newton's theory describes, especially the planetary orbits, but also the effect of gravity upon light – a problem area about which Newton had nothing to say either in his theory of gravitation or in his optics. Einstein's theory is thus more risky. It may in principle be falsified by observations that do not touch Newton's theory. The empirical content of Einstein's theory, its quantity of potential falsifiers, is thus considerably greater than the empirical content of Newton's theory. Finally, the potential explanatory power of Einstein's theory is by far the greater. If, for instance, we accept that such optical effects as Einstein's predicted redshift in the spectrum of the satellite of Sirius have been confirmed by observations, then these optical effects are also *explained* by Einstein's theory.

But even if the relevant observations have not yet been made, we can say that Einstein's theory is *potentially* superior to Newton's. It has the greater empirical content and the greater explanatory potential. This means that it is theoretically more interesting. At the same time, however, Einstein's theory is at much greater *risk* than Newton's. It is much more prone to falsification, precisely because the number of its potential falsifiers is greater.

It is therefore much more rigorously testable than Newton's theory, which is itself already very rigorously testable. If Einstein's theory stands up to these tests, if it proves its mettle, we still cannot say that it is true, for it may be falsified in later testing; but we can say that not only its empirical content but also its truth content is greater than those of Newton's theory. This means that the number of *true* statements that can be derived from it is greater than the number that can be derived from Newton's theory. And we can say further that Einstein's theory, in light of the critical discussion that makes full use of results of experimental tests, appears to be a better *approximation to the truth*.

The idea of approximation to the truth – like the idea of truth as a regulative principle – presupposes a *realistic view of the world*. It does *not* presuppose that reality is as our scientific theories describe it; but it does presuppose that there is a reality and that we and our theories – which are ideas we have ourselves created and are therefore always idealizations – can draw closer and closer to an adequate description of reality, if we employ the four-stage method of trial and error. But the method is not enough. We must also be lucky. For the conditions we find here on earth, which make life possible and also the development of human speech, human consciousness, and human science, are extremely rare in the cosmos, even if the cosmos is a long way from being as science describes it. For according to science, the world is almost empty of matter and is mainly filled with chaotic radiation; and in the few places where it is *not* empty, it is filled with *chaotic* matter, usually much too hot for the formation of molecules or too cold for the development of forms of life as we know it. Whether or not there is life elsewhere in the universe, from a cosmological point of view life is an uncommonly rare, quite extraordinary phenomenon. And in the development of life, the critical scientific method is in turn an uncommonly rare development – on any probability calculation, almost infinitely improbable. This means that we hit the jackpot when life and science came into being.

The *realistic view of the world*, together with the idea of approximation to the *truth*, seem to me indispensable for an understanding of the perpetually *idealizing* character of science. Moreover, the realistic view of the world seems to me the only humane world-view: it alone accounts for the fact that there are other people who live, suffer, and die as we do.

Science is a system of the products of human ideas – so far idealism is right. But these ideas are likely to fail when tested against reality. This is why realism is right in the end.

I may be thought for a moment to have gone outside my topic with these remarks on realism and the dispute between realism and idealism. But this is not the case – on the contrary. The realism dispute is highly topical in quantum mechanics, and is thus one of the most up-to-date and most open problems in philosophy of science today.

It will be clear by now that I do not have a neutral attitude to this problem. I am totally on the side of *realism*. But there is an influential idealist school in quantum mechanics. In fact there are all conceivable idealist shades, and one famous quantum physicist has even drawn *solipsistic* consequences from quantum mechanics; he claims that these solipsistic consequences necessarily follow from quantum mechanics.

All I can say in reply is that if this is so, something must be wrong with quantum mechanics, however admirable it may be, and however excellent it is as an approximation to reality. Quantum mechanics has stood up to exceptionally rigorous testing. But from this we can draw conclusions about its proximity to the truth only if we are realists.

The struggle over realism and objectivism in scientific theory will continue for a long time to come. We are dealing here with an open and topical problem. It is also, as has been well said, a problem that in a sense carries scientific theory beyond itself. I hope I have made my own position sufficiently clear on this fundamental problem.

Notes

1 John Eccles, *The Physiology of Synapses*, Springer Verlag, Heidelberg, 1964.
2 John Eccles, *Facing Reality: Adventures of a Brain Scientist*, Springer Verlag, New York, Heidelberg & Berlin, 1970, pp. 105–106.

2

NOTES OF A REALIST
ON THE BODY–MIND
PROBLEM*

As far as I can recall, my lecture here is only the third I have given in Germany. It is certainly the first in Mannheim. I do not come here all that often, and so I have had to choose my topic carefully.

I

Originally I thought of speaking today about my first book, about the solution of the two basic problems of epistemology: that is, first, the problem of demarcating between empirical science and other thoroughly meaningful and important fields such as metaphysics; and second, the problem of induction. But my solution to these problems is familiar and available in my book *The Logic of Scientific Discovery*; and although I have some new and hitherto unpublished results, I was afraid of giving the impression that even in old age I have not gone beyond the issues with which I started out.

Then I also thought of speaking about a topic in social philosophy. But three volumes of mine in this area too have been translated into German, and it is a field in which my friend Professor Hans Albert has said many excellent things in his brilliant book *Traktat über die kritische Vernunft*.[1]

I have yet other reasons for choosing the problem of the interaction between body and mind. This problem includes a major puzzle that can perhaps never be solved. Indeed it is the deepest and most difficult problem of philosophy, the central problem of modern metaphysics.

* Lecture given in Mannheim, 8 May 1972.

And it is of the utmost significance for us humans. It is the basis of what modern existentialism likes to call *the human situation*, for man is a spiritual being, at least as long as he is fully conscious. He is a spiritual being, an ego, a mind that is most closely bound up with a body subject to the laws of physics. This is almost *too* self-evident to express, and existentialists have accepted the problems lying behind this self-evidence – I should like to say, behind this overwhelming self-evidence – without even attempting to say something rational by way of explanation.

But the problem of the body–mind relationship is a serious problem. It includes the problem of human freedom, which in every respect, including politics, is a fundamental problem; and it includes the problem of man's position in the physical world, the physical cosmos, a world that I shall later describe as 'World 1'. The world of conscious human processes I shall call 'World 2', and the world of the objective creations of the human mind I shall call 'World 3'. More about this later.

Here I should like just briefly to mention another reason why I chose this topic and already presented myself in the title as a realist. Many philosophers and sociologists in Germany who know my work only by hearsay describe me as a 'positivist', because my first book – which, as a matter of fact, sharply criticized the positivism of the Vienna Circle – appeared in a series of volumes published by this same Vienna Circle. In that context, to be a 'positivist' is tantamount to being an opponent of all philosophical speculation and especially an opponent of *realism*. One of the reasons that led me to choose today's topic is that I wanted to choose one that is *non-positivistic* in its very title.

One more remark about the word 'metaphysics'. Hegel, Marx, Engels, and Lenin use this word to denote a philosophy *hostile to evolution*, which sees the world as *static* instead of seeing it as dynamic. This usage was always highly questionable, since the *problem of change* and the unceasing evolution of the world was one of the oldest problems of pre-Socratic metaphysics. At any event, I do not believe in a static world but in a world that is changing; and as far as I know, it is a long time since there has been a metaphysician in that static sense. I think of myself, then, as a metaphysical realist who accepts the theory of evolution and who, I should perhaps add, introduced the dynamic problem of the growth of our knowledge into the philosophy of science.

For the final point in this introduction, I should like to say that I attach the greatest value to expressing myself in a simple, generally intelligible manner. But unfortunately this does not mean that my remarks can be very easily understood. The hardest part is to distinguish World 1, World 2, and especially World 3. I shall begin with this difficulty. Everything further will then be comparatively easy.

I call the world of physical events 'World 1', and the world of mental events 'World 2'. That is relatively straightforward. The difficulty begins with what I call 'World 3'.

In the broadest sense 'World 3' is the world of products of the human mind; in the narrow sense it is the world of theories, including false theories, and the world of scientific problems, including questions to do with the truth or falsity of various theories. In the broad sense, literary and artistic works such as Mozart's operas and concertos belong to World 3. But if you like, the world of artistic works can also be called World 4. That is a terminological question.

The important thing is to distinguish World 3 of scientific theories from problems of the psychological World 2. The distinction was made most clearly by Bernard Bolzano and later by Gottlob Frege; but, as I shall explain, I go beyond both of them.

Bolzano spoke of the world of 'statements in themselves'. By this he meant statements in the logical sense, in contrast to the psychological thought processes that occur when we think a statement. Frege spoke of the *content* of a statement, by which he too meant a statement in the logical sense.

Let us take a simple example. Two mathematicians come to the wrong conclusion that $3 \times 4 = 13$. Here are two thought processes in World 2, processes that may be very different from each other. But '3 $\times 4 = 13$' is only *one* statement in itself (which is false), only *one* (logically false) *content*. This statement in itself belongs not to World 2 but to World 3. We can say of it that it logically contradicts the statement '$3 \times 4 = 12$'. We can also say that this statement, $3 \times 4 = 13$, belongs to World 3 because it is and always will be objectively false, even if many great mathematicians were to believe it.

We can therefore distinguish between World 2, in which subjective *thought processes* are to be found, and World 3, in which objective statements or objective *thought contents* are to be found.

These are, essentially, the views of Bolzano and Frege. I go beyond them by admitting into World 3 not only true statements in themselves but also false statements in themselves, as well as *problems* and *arguments*.

Here I would like to say two things in particular about World 3: first, that it is real; and second, that it is at least partly autonomous, that it has an internal structure that is at least partly independent of World 2.

Let us first speak of its reality. The paradigms of all reality are the physical *objects* of World 1: stones, trees, animals. In addition, I propose to call 'real' something that is capable of having an *effect*, either direct or indirect, upon the *objects* of World 1.

I now claim that scientific theories, which belong to World 3, can have a direct or indirect effect upon the things of World 1.

The simplest examples may be found in the construction of skyscrapers. A skyscraper is a physical object; it belongs to World 1. But it is built according to a plan, and the plan is affected by theories and by a large number of problems.

I admit that the plans, theories, and problems that can play a role in the construction of a skyscraper initially have an effect upon the consciousness of people such as architects – on World 2, therefore – and only later upon the world of the physical movements of construction workers, and hence upon physical excavators, stone, and brick. This is the most frequent case: World 3 usually has an indirect effect upon World 1, via the mental World 2. Perhaps it is not only mostly but always the case that World 3 affects World 1 not directly but *only* via World 2. At any event, our example shows the *reality of all three worlds*, not only World 1 but also World 2 and World 3.

If a skyscraper or a bridge collapses – which unfortunately happens now and then – this is sometimes attributable to a World 2 error in thought, a false subjective belief, but sometimes also to a false objective *theory*, to an error in World 3.

Of course, there are philosophers who deny the reality of World 3: they say that our thoughts, and therefore World 2, do exist, but not the contents in themselves. They regard these merely as mental abstractions, as fantasies of the brain.

The view I shall defend here is that World 3 is certainly the genetic product of World 2, but that it has a partly autonomous internal structure.

Some good examples come from mathematics. The series of natural numbers 1, 2, 3, 4 . . . and so on is, I think, a product of our language. There are primitive languages that know only '1, 2 and many', and others in which you can count only up to 5.

The infinite series of natural numbers is (like human language in general) a great invention of man. But no one invented the *prime numbers*: they were *discovered* in the sequence of counting.

I must develop this important point a little.

The great German mathematician Kronecker said of mathematics: the natural numbers were created by God – everything else is man's work. I say, on the other hand: the natural numbers are man's work;

they are a by-product of human language, of the invention of counting on and on. Addition is also a human invention, as is multiplication.

But the *laws* of addition and multiplication (the associative laws, for example) are not a human invention. They are unintended consequences of human invention, and they were *discovered*. And the existence of *prime numbers* – indivisible numbers that are the product only of themselves and unity – is also a discovery, no doubt quite a late one. The prime numbers were discovered in the series of natural numbers, not by everyone but by people who studied these numbers and their special peculiarities – by real mathematicians.

Historically, it may be said that they were invented along with the natural numbers; but they did not exist in World 2 of human consciousness before they were discovered, certainly many hundreds of years later. We can say that they immediately existed in World 3 together with the natural numbers: they therefore existed in an *autonomous* part of World 3 *before* they were discovered. *After* their discovery, they existed both in World 2 (though only for a small group of people, for mathematicians) and in World 3.

We can, indeed must, say that the existence of the prime numbers in World 3 was one of the causes of the thought processes within World 2 that led to their discovery – just as the existence of Mount Everest was a cause that led the Indian land survey office to discover it. This shows that the autonomous part of World 3 can have a causal effect upon World 2. But the autonomous part of World 3 thereby also acts upon World 1. The first mathematician who explained to his colleagues that there are prime numbers doubtless used his tongue to do this. But our tongues, like the rest of our bodies, belong to World 1.

Later mathematicians began to study the prime numbers more closely, and such investigations have still not been completed. There are a lot of *open problems* in the theory of numbers. These problems were also discovered; they belong to the autonomous part of World 3.

The ancient mathematicians found, for example, that prime numbers generally occur less and less often, or lie less and less closely together, as we advance in the series to larger and larger numbers. The series of prime numbers begins with 2, 3, 5, 7; 2 and 3 are the only pair of prime numbers so close to each other that no natural number comes between them. But there are many pairs of prime numbers – for example, 5 and 7, 11 and 13, 17 and 19, 29 and 31 – that are so close to each other that they are separated by only *one* other number. These may be called the twin prime numbers.

I shall now mention a few problems that have been discovered in World 3 concerning prime numbers.

First problem. As we keep advancing and prime numbers become rarer and rarer, does there come a point beyond which they peter out altogether? Or in other words, is there or is there not a greatest *prime number*, after which there are only composite numbers?

The problem may already have been posed *before* Euclid, but anyway it was he who solved it. Euclid discovered a proof that there is *no such thing as the greatest* prime number. He thus showed that the series of prime numbers has no end, just as the series of natural numbers has no end. For the series of natural numbers the proof is very simple. Let us assume that it has an end and that the number *a* is the greatest natural number. If we then simply construct the number *a* + *1*, this shows that our assumption was wrong. We have here a simple *reductio ad absurdum* of the assumption that there is a greatest natural number. Euclid invented a rather more complicated *reductio ad absurdum* of the assumption that there is a *greatest prime number*. This wonderfully beautiful proof of Euclid's thus establishes a theorem: that the series of prime numbers is infinite. This theorem belongs to World 3. Euclid's imaginative work belongs to World 2; and it causally depends upon the World 3 fact that *there really is no greatest prime number*.

Euclid wrote down the proof in his famous book *The Elements*. The World 3 theorem was thus committed to papyrus, so that it causally modified World 1 via the World 2 of the human Euclid. Euclid's beautiful proof is now in every printed book on number theory. But a book is printed with machines. These machines, as well as the books, are physical objects that plainly belong to World 1. Again we have a *causal* effect that starts from the autonomous part of World 3 and then causally affects World 1 via World 2.

Another similar, but to my knowledge still *unsolved*, problem is whether there is a greatest pair of twin prime numbers. To my knowledge, no mathematician doubts that there is no greatest pair of twin primes. But as far as I am aware, there is no proof of this assumption. It is an unsolved problem of World 3, and it has a causal effect upon all mathematicians striving to solve it.

I have just said that books belong to World 1. But of course, their *content* belongs to World 3. Two different editions of Euclid's *Elements* both belong to World 1, insofar as they are different; but they belong to World 3 insofar as they have the *same content*.

Books, libraries, and the manuscript of my lecture therefore belong to World 1 and to World 3. If someone in the audience does not understand German – perhaps I should say, my somewhat Viennese German – then he hears only the acoustic aspect of my lecture, the aspect that belongs to World 1. But for anyone who understands German and makes the effort to follow my arguments, only the aspect of my lecture that belongs to World 3 is important.

Your effort to follow the content of my lecture belongs to World 2. If you make the effort, you concentrate on an object that belongs to World 3. Your World 2 is thus causally influenced by World 3.

There are objects, then, that belong to both World 1 and World 3, and objects that belong to both World 2 and World 3. My main thesis is that there are also objects that belong *only* to *World 3* – for example, *a yet undiscovered proof* on which a mathematician is working today and which he will discover tomorrow. The proof will tomorrow belong to both World 2 and World 3, and if it is written down, to World 1 as well. (But it already today influences World 2.)

We do not know, but we may suppose that the proof already belongs to World 1 before it is written down. For the thought processes in World 2 are presumably bound up with events in the brain, and thus with physical events in World 1.

II

This brings me to the body–mind problem.

The body–mind problem is the question of whether and how our thought processes in World 2 are bound up with brain events in World 1.

The main attempts at a solution are the following.

1   *Body–mind interaction*: World 2 and World 1 interact, so that when someone reads a book or listens to a lecture, brain events occur that *act* upon the World 2 of the reader's or listener's thoughts; and conversely, when a mathematician follows a proof, his World 2 *acts* upon his brain and thus upon World 1. This, then, is the thesis of body–mind interaction.

2   *Body–mind parallelism*: each thought process in World 2 runs parallel to a brain event in World 1.

3   *Pure physicalism or philosophical behaviourism*: there is only one world, namely, World 1, and in it there are movements by men and animals, or human and animal behaviour. In this view, what I call World 2 simply does not exist, and certainly not what I call World 3.

4   *Pure mentalism or spiritualism*: only World 2 exists and World 1 is only my idea.

Essentially, then, we have these four attempted solutions: (1) body–mind interaction; (2) body–mind parallelism; (3) pure physicalism or philosophical behaviourism; (4) pure mentalism.

I would argue that the first and oldest of these attempted solutions is the only one that deserves to be taken seriously.

Let us briefly look at the third and fourth attempted solutions. I maintain that both are typical of attempts to solve a problem through a kind of head-in-the-sand philosophy. The problem of the body–mind relation vanishes into triviality as soon as one denies the existence of either the body or the mind.

I could show in detail that the logical structure of these two attempted solutions is such a head-in-the-sand philosophy. Although pure physicalism or behaviourism currently has many supporters, especially among British, American, and Australian philosophers, I cannot take them seriously enough to spend my time on a detailed critique.

My discussion of the existence of World 3 mainly involves arguments that, in my view, establish the existence of World 2 as an intermediary between World 3 and World 1.

Much the same may be said of pure mentalism. We know today that there is no material *substance*, because matter has a highly complex and already partly clarified *structure*. (A substance, in philosophy, is an unanalysed bearer of essential properties that explain but neither require nor are capable of explanation.) Although matter is not a substance, *material things* are the best examples of things that we regard as real or existent.

So much for solutions 3 and 4. The situation is different with the second attempted solution, body–mind parallelism.

Body-mind parallelism recognizes the existence of body and mind and might even accept the existence of World 3. From the point of view of the body–mind problem, the main motive for parallelism is that it allows the world to be seen as causally self-contained or, more precisely, as consisting of two parallel, causally self-contained systems.

This is especially important *for any physicist*, since the idea that physical events may depend upon mental events is quite repulsive to a physicist. Moreover, it is difficult to come up with a model of such a causal effect, that is, to conceive of it in every detail.

This is the real reason that has led people to reject body–mind interaction.

I come now to counter-arguments. I readily admit that there are no mental processes without events in the brain. But to speak of parallelism, we would also have to say that there is a part of the brain where no physical events occur without causing parallel mental events.

What is more, we would have to say that there is a one-to-one relationship between *all* characteristic events in that part of the brain and *all* characteristic events in World 2.

But there does not seem to be such a one-to-one relationship. One can remove parts of the brain, and other parts take over their function. The possibility of a *transfer of functions* seems in general to be characteristic of *most living creatures* (and most phenomena in life). And although I am willing to accept that there are no thought processes in World 2 without some brain events in World 1, everything suggests to me that no real parallelism occurs. It is rather like the relationship between a thought *content* in World 3 and its materialization in World 1 – say, in a book or a lecture. My own lecture here remains the same in a World 3 sense, whether my delivery is fast or slow, loud or soft. It can also be translated fairly precisely into another language. And a book may be printed very differently in various editions. Of course, the different printings and translations all have something in common; but there is no one-to-one correspondence, and therefore no real parallelism.

Now I come to my most important argument. Please consider how much our physical environment, World 1, has changed as a result of World 3 theories – for instance, atomic theory or Hertzian waves (that is, the theory of radio transmission, so important for the control of moon rockets). If we look in this way at World 1 and especially *changes* in World 1, then it seems quite clear to me that the physical world is not causally isolated from World 2 and World 3.

Yet the attempt to save World 1's causal closure is, logically speaking, the main reason why the first and oldest attempted solution, body–mind interaction, is replaced with parallelism (or even pure physicalism).

This attempt strikes me as unrealistic. And although, as a former student and teacher of physics, I can well see why it is so hard to admit that physics is not causally self-contained, this ideology seems to me to be refuted by the facts.

The ideology of the causal closure of the physical world stems from a time when mechanics was the whole of physics. This ideology is already refuted by the necessity of adding a theory of electromagnetism.

We know nothing about the connection between electromagnetic forces and gravitation, or between these two areas of physics and nuclear forces. We have no mechanical 'model' for these connections; yet it cannot be doubted that these different areas stand in a relationship of interaction – that, for example, gravitational pressure in the sun triggers the action of nuclear forces which, in turn, convert hydrogen atoms into helium atoms. Nevertheless, it does not appear that the different forces – gravity, electromagnetism, nuclear forces – can be directly reduced to one another. None of these areas is self-contained, although the ideology of causal closure has spawned numerous attempts to find a unitary theory. Einstein worked on this from 1919 to 1955. In these circumstances, it seems wrong to me to stick dogmatically to the causal closure of physics.

To summarize: the fact that our theories, which belong to World 3, have an effect on World 1 via World 2 counts against the thesis of the causal closure of World 1. But then no objections remain *against* the theory of body–mind interaction.

III

My next point is the following. The existence of World 3, and the fact that we can grasp World 3 objects through *thought processes in World 2*, play a crucial role in accounting for human self-consciousness, for self-awareness and for the human mind, as distinct from the animal mind.

I have already said that matter is not a substance but has an unusually complex structure, which is at least partly open to *explanation*. In the same way, the human mind, the human self, is not a substance but an unusually complex structure.

First of all, it does not consist merely of consciousness: it is always accompanied by knowledge rooted in World 3 theories.

Animals too have expectations bound up with past experiences. I am sure you know the story of the rat who said to another rat: 'I've trained my man in a white coat so well that he brings me something to eat whenever I press this lever.' I think this story is much closer to the truth than the theory of conditioned reflexes, which I don't believe in. Pavlov's dog certainly has reflexes, but it is not conditioned: it makes *discoveries*. Unfortunately I cannot go into this here. Anyway, animals have dispositional knowledge as well as an awareness of time. But we can conjecture that they do not have a theory of time – of past, present, and future. For self-consciousness, however, it is essential for me to know that I have a *life history* that can be reconstructed at least in broad outline. We know there are pathological states in which someone can forget who he is. It follows that knowledge of one's own identity is not simply a matter of course. I do not doubt that there is an innate disposition to develop self-consciousness or a self. But we need *social interaction with others*, and above all we need *to learn a language* and *theories expressed in language*, if we are to learn that we have a self.

Animals can have a character or a personality, which is partly dispositional and perhaps also partly learnt. But I do not think an animal is conscious of its identity. Relevant here, among other things, are the theory that we are the same before falling asleep and after waking up (that is, the theory of the genidentity of physical bodies), and the theory that we all have a body; and, in addition, the theory that our consciousness is often interrupted by sleep, but that our body remains the same and we can summon up thoughts we have had in recent days and remember our waking states. This is much more than mere recollection in the sense that animals also recollect. I suspect that, for fully developed self-consciousness, there must be a language in which we can refer to others and ourselves by name. It is no accident that children learn to say their own names before they refer to themselves with the word 'I'.

So there is exceptionally important interaction between the World 3 of theories and the human World 2 of conscious processes; and my thesis is that the self-consciousness characteristic of humans can develop *only* through this interaction.

IV

The theory I have briefly sketched here is intimately bound up with my theory of knowledge and my theory of science.

The underlying idea of my theory of knowledge is that *problems* and *attempts to solve them through hypotheses, theories, or conjectures* precede all observation. Logically as well as historically, theories come first in our experience of the world – first both in our personal history and in the history of humanity.

What correspond to theories at a prehuman level are dispositions and expectations. Magic and ritual probably have close antecedents in the animal realm. What we humans have in addition is the speech form of *story-telling*.

The novelty in human language is that it can describe and argue. Already among animals there are expressions of inner states, and signals such as warnings and threats.

I imagine that the invention of *distinctively human language* is connected with the possibility of *reporting* or recounting what has happened. Subsequently, reports often become tinged with wishes. Stories start to be told, and as these often contradict one another a problem of truth arises – the problem of whether a tale or report (about a hunt, for example) is true or false. With the problem of whether an account is true or merely wishful boasting (as in fishermen's tales), the decisively important problem of truth makes its appearance. At the same time, the telling of fairy tales or stories becomes possible. Such tales or stories or myths are also the original theoretical explanations: the beginnings of science among the Greeks go back to Homer and Hesiod; the beginnings of art, the prehistoric cave paintings of hunting and animals, are magical stories; Egyptian and Assyrian art largely comprises illustrations of stories or of contemporary events. This is how World 3 began to develop.

To conclude. My emphasis on the theoretical character of human knowledge has led me from epistemology to the theory of World 3. I do think that our humanity is rooted in the existence of World 3, that it can be explained only in connection with an objective World 3 and the idea of the creation of myths as well as of objective truth.

Summary

In my lecture I have tried to do the following.

1   I have *not* tried to solve the body–mind problem: that is, I do not know how the brain and consciousness act upon each other.
2   But I have posed the problem in a *new* way that is *different* from how it is usually presented.
3   I stress the existence of three partly autonomous but interacting worlds: a physical World 1, a World 2 of conscious processes, and a World 3 of products of the human mind.
4   I have tried to show, especially against physicalism or behaviourism, that World 2 exists because it alone can account for the influence of World 3 upon World 1.
5   I have tried to show that the physical World 1 is open to the mental World 2. This is a thesis that physicists are very reluctant to accept. But I have tried to show that it nevertheless appears to be true.
6   I have especially tried to show that World 2 connects or interacts with World 3 so closely that human self-consciousness is incomprehensible without the existence of World 3. Self-consciousness is anchored in World 3.

7　Genetically, then, the human World 2 is as much a product of World 3 as World 3 is a product of World 2. Or to put it in another way: we are a product of our products, of the civilization to which we all contribute.

Note

1　*Treatise on Critical Reason*, Princeton University Press, 1982.

3

EPISTEMOLOGY AND
THE PROBLEM OF PEACE*

I

May I say that I am very happy to see the unexpectedly large number of young people here? I plan to undertake quite a long and adventurous journey with you, and so perhaps I should first introduce myself.

Today, at eighty-three years of age, I am the happiest person I know. I find life indescribably wonderful. It is undoubtedly also terrible, and I have experienced painfully sad deaths among my close relations and friends. Sixteen of my close relatives fell victim to Hitler, some in Auschwitz, some by suicide. But despite everything, although I was desperate more than once and still today have grave worries, although for me it has been up one minute and down the next, I am happy.

I will not spend much longer on myself. What I feel is stated well in the first eight lines of the Prologue in Heaven in Goethe's *Faust*. I see the world as he does:

> Die Sonne tönt nach alter Weise
> In Brudersphären Wettgesang,
> Und ihre vorgeschriebne Reise
> Vollendet sie mit Donnergang.
> Ihr Anblick gibt den Engeln Stärke,
> Wenn keiner sie ergründen mag:
> Die unbegreiflich hohen Werke
> Sind herrlich wie am ersten Tag.[1]

* A lecture delivered in Zurich, August 1985.

I say all this because I consider the current dominant ideology among intellectuals – of the wickedness of our world – to be a foolishness and a false religion. Men are terribly in need of suggestion, and this dangerous need for suggestion is one of my main themes today. My theme is large. I have worked hard but gladly to present it as simply as I can. I fear I have not fully succeeded, and I must ask for your active cooperation.

But I would also ask you not to believe *anything* that I suggest! Please do not believe a word! I know that that is asking too much, as I will speak only the truth, as well as I can. But I warn you: I know *nothing*, or *almost nothing*. We all know nothing or almost nothing. I *conjecture* that that is a basic fact of life. We know nothing, we can only conjecture: we guess. Our best knowledge is the wonderful scientific knowledge we have built up over 2,500 years. But the natural sciences consist precisely of conjectures or hypotheses.

In Greek, Latin, English, and German there is a clear distinction between

(1) *Wissen* [knowledge] ≠ *Vermutung* [conjecture]
     ich weiß [I know] ≠ *ich vermute* [I conjecture].

The distinction is quite simple:

(2) *Wissen* implies *certain truth*
     thus: *Wissen* implies *sureness* or *certainty*.

In these languages you cannot seriously say: 'I *know* today is Friday, but I'm not quite sure.' The rejoinder would be: 'If you're not quite sure, you don't *know* it but only conjecture it.'

My first thesis, then, is:

(3) *So-called scientific knowledge is not knowledge*, for it consists only of conjectures or hypotheses – even if some have gone through the crossfire of ingenious tests. In short:

(4) We do not know, we guess. Although *scientific knowledge* is not knowledge, it is the best we have in this field. I call it conjectural knowledge – more or less to console people who want certain knowledge and think they cannot do without it.

Such people have a dangerous need for suggestion, they lack the *courage* to live *without assurances, without certainty, without authority, without a leader*. Perhaps one could say that they are people still trapped in childhood.

Others may need friends and confidants, or people they look up to as a model or as having achieved something out of the ordinary. If they are looking after a sick person, they may often long for an authority (a medical authority). But there is none; for knowledge – certain knowledge – is an empty word.

Science is the quest for truth. But truth is not *certain* truth.

(5)   *Truth ≠ certain truth*
      Truth ≠ certainty.

Everyone knows what truth is. It is the correspondence of a statement with the reality about which the statement says something:

(6)   Truth = correspondence with reality, or perhaps
      Truth = correspondence of the alleged facts with the
      actual facts.

But definitions are not important. And quibbling over words is a menace.

(7) We can assert the truth, attain the truth, often enough. But we can never attain certainty. For we know – in the sense of conjectural knowledge – that there are people with a delusion that they are Einstein or a reincarnation of Goethe. So presumably I speak the truth when I say that I am just now giving a lecture in Zurich. But from my experience of such people, I cannot be absolutely sure that I am not caught up in some similarly terrible mistake.

Now, only absolute certainty would mean genuine knowledge. We never get beyond conjectures – except perhaps with trivialities – at least not in the natural sciences. (It is perhaps different in mathematics or in formal logic, but I shall not speak of them today.)

Science is the quest for truth, *not* for certainty. How does it work?

(8) Scientists, like all organisms, work with the method of trial and error. The trial is a *solution to a problem*. In the evolution of the plant or animal kingdom, error or, to be more precise, the correction of error usually means eradication of the organism; in science it usually means eradication of the hypothesis or theory.

The process is thus one of *Darwinian selection*. Question: What in the animal realm corresponds to so-called knowledge, to conjecture or hypothesis? Answer: *expectation*. Or more precisely: a state of the organism in which it prepares for a change (or no change) in its surroundings. When flowers are in bud, they are in this sense *expecting* spring weather: they have incorporated the hypothesis or theory that it is getting warmer. Often enough the theory is false, and the blossom is killed by frost.

(9) In this sense there is an infinite amount of innate knowledge in plants and animals. A baby expects to be cared for and nursed, and soon to be smiled at. Not only does it expect these things, it needs them. Inborn needs are inborn theories.

(10) All organisms are all the time highly active. They actively investigate their environment, look for better living conditions, for a better world. And they themselves actively improve their conditions of life.

(11) Life improves the environment for life. It has been doing that for millions of years, and we are the fortunate inheritors.

Since this process takes place through trial and (the elimination of) error, there are also many mistakes in our world.

(12) Problems arise together with life; and there are problems only when there are values: for example, evaluations of living conditions.

Now I am coming to the end of what I wanted to explain about the theory of knowledge and the philosophy of science.

(13) Science begins with problems. It *attempts* to solve them through bold, inventive theories. The great majority of theories are false and/or untestable. Valuable, testable theories will search for errors. We try to find errors and to eliminate them. This is science: it consists of wild, often irresponsible ideas that it places under the strict control of error correction.

Question: This is the same process as in amoebas and other lower organisms. What is the difference between an amoeba and Einstein? Answer: The amoeba is eliminated when it *makes* mistakes. If it is conscious it will be afraid of mistakes. Einstein *looks for* mistakes. He is able to do this because his theory is not part of himself but an object he can consciously investigate and criticize. He owes this to *specifically* human language, and especially to its offspring, human writing. Einstein said somewhere: 'My pencil is more intelligent than I.' What is expressed, or even better what is written down, has become an object we can criticize and investigate for mistakes. A theory formulated in language thus becomes something similar to, but also quite different from, expectations, which are part of all plants and animals.

(14) The method of natural science is the conscious search for errors and correction of them through conscious criticism. Ideally such criticism should be impersonal and directed only at the theories or hypotheses in question.

This brings me to the end of my remarks on the theory of

knowledge. I turn now to the theory of animal language and specifi-cally human language, which is the second part of my lecture. The third part deals with the inborn need for implicit guidance, and the fourth part with the problem of peace.

II

I shall begin with a model that I owe to the great psychologist Karl Bühler. Bühler distinguishes three functions of speech. The first two are found among many animals and all humans, the third only among humans.

The lowest function is the function of expression, which may con-sist in facial gestures, tail movements or various forms of calling. These expressive movements may be regarded as symptoms of the inner state of the organism.

(Incidental remark. Materialists and behaviourists are not keen on this. They will not accept any inner state, but propose to limit them-selves to *behaviour*. But it can soon be shown that this is a mistake. A thermometer displays by its 'behaviour' not only the external tem-perature but above all its inner state: oscillating molecules with increasing amplitudes result in the lengthening of a column of metal. If behaviourist ideology were correct, we could not appeal to these inner states but should simply explain the lengthening of the column as an effect of heating.)

An animal may express its state through movements of its face or tail, even if no other animal is there to react to it. But if another animal does react, the expressive movement becomes a signal. This 'announcement function', the second in Bühler's model, may be a signalling function, and if it is reciprocal we have communication between animals. Of course, communication at this level also takes place between humans – for example, infants before they have learnt a human language, or people who have no specifically human language in common but try to make themselves understood through facial expressions, signs, or pointing.

Bühler's third function, the function of representation [*Darstellung*], is unique to specifically human language, in which there are statements that describe or, as Bühler puts it, represent facts.

One of Bühler's theses is that the higher function is always accom-panied by the lower. When a bird gives a warning cry, this serves not only as a means of social communication but also as an expression of an inner state. The higher we go in the functions of language, the more complex the language becomes.

I should point out briefly that only a few theorists of language have gone as far as Bühler. Most speak of expression, and some of social communication (which may naturally have very practical functions, as the example of the warning cry shows). Commands or invitations also belong in this category. But very few have seen that what is decisive for human language and its many wonders is that it can describe facts and that such descriptive statements may be either true or false. Only through this huge step forward can the utterance become objective and factual criticism begin. Criticism is rational only when it concerns the truth or falsity of statements or theories.

Here I shall end my brief presentation of an important part of Bühler's theory of language.

I myself have added a few functions of language to Bühler's – above all, the *critical function*, that is, critical discussion of the truth or falsity of propositions. And I also stressed its huge importance when I spoke of how Einstein differs from an amoeba.

In fact, I have often stressed that the *critical stage* of human language must logically be preceded by a *dogmatic* stage. Only when a dogma is established as a kind of background can one begin to criticize, and only later can the dogma – the background of critical discussion – itself be included in the criticism. First there needs to be a solid framework. Later one can contrast a number of such frameworks and pass on to critical discussion of them.

III

Now I come to the third part.

I shall begin with my fifteenth thesis.

(15) Animal languages, including human languages, presuppose a large number of inborn needs: for example, the need for active self-expression, the need to engage in communication with others, and the need to learn by trial and error in these matters too. Without such inborn needs, and without active learning through trial and error (the scampering of kittens is a good example), it would not be possible for higher animals to survive.

(16) The innate knowledge of animals and humans, as well as knowledge acquired through active learning, consists of *expectations*. Unfulfilled expectations are experienced as difficulties or problems, which lead again to experiments, to active learning – to research.

(17) Active learning of both animal and human language assumes a very high degree of suggestibility. The ability to copy is *not* enough. More is involved even than in copying plus empathy, although that is

getting closer. We are talking now of a deep inborn need to agree with the wishes and evaluations of other communicating members of the same species. Only this can explain the mass migration of herrings or the swarming of bees or even a swarming of mosquitoes. And we know (in the sense of conjectural knowledge) how suggestible certain animals are. A chicken can be hypnotized by a chalk line.

(18) Human languages rest upon inborn needs to learn a language, to speak, to describe, to communicate. They are largely the result of an inborn need, connected with language, to be guided by suggestion.

(19) All this is very closely connected to our strong need to discover the world around us, to learn about it and thus *to know*. Human groups create myths, medicine-men, and priests. In due course an inner conflict arises that may reinforce this need, an unacknowledged feeling that we really know nothing or only very little. As there is a strong need for security – or for assurance by comrades and helpers – the need will also be strong to have a *common dogma* and to suggest the truth of the dogma to one another. It is a need for implicit guidance.[2] Uncertainty is feared, and dogma becomes fanatical belief.

This is how the war psychosis, the war fever, came about at the beginning of the First World War.

But before I come to the topic of war and peace, may I say a few words about art – and about modern art.

We all know that the greatest art is religious art: the cathedrals, the Sistine Chapel, the *St Matthew Passion*, the masses of Mozart, Beethoven, and Schubert.

How does religious art fare today?

I think a great deal is explained if we assume that a false religion has established itself today: namely, the religion that our world, at least our social world, is a hell.

I am anything but an enemy of religion. My religion is the doctrine of the splendours of the world; of the freedom and creativity of wonderful human beings; of the terror and suffering of the despairing people we can help; of the extent of good and evil that has emerged in human history and keeps emerging over and over again; of the joyful message that we can prolong people's lives, especially those of women and children who have had the toughest life. I know nothing else. And although the scientific *quest* for truth is part of my religion, the magnificent scientific *hypotheses* are not religion. They must not be.

But modern art is explained by this crazy belief of the modern religion: by the belief in the wickedness of the world and of the social order in which we are supposed to live in Switzerland, Germany, Britain, and North America. Everywhere young people are talked into believing –

and shown with intellectualistic arguments and with the help of modern art – that they live in a hell. What are the consequences? Children actually do need leaders and models, dogmas, and a firm routine. Later, as adolescents, they can and should begin to free themselves of the leaders, dogmas, and 'all-knowing' ideologies. Indeed that is quite easy. Just don't let yourselves be talked into believing anything – not by me either, of course. From any history book you can learn for yourselves whether our own age, which has abolished slavery, is not the best age of which we have historical knowledge. Of course we have made and continue to make many mistakes – through our appalling ideologies, for example.

The Russians, who live in an otherwise much worse world, suggest to their children and young people that their country is paradise. The fact is that this helps. The Russians are more contented than we are. The need for suggestion is a great power. But so is the truth when one is struggling for it.

IV

I have been trying to show the epistemological, biological, and linguistic roots of our dangerous susceptibility to dogmas and ideologies. One of the roots of this susceptibility is, quite simply, cowardice. Now, I too am cowardly, and I would not like to feign unusual courage or urge anyone on to heroic deeds. But I shall stress that the great problem of establishing perpetual peace on earth is not unsolvable.

This is the theme of Kant's book *On Perpetual Peace*. It is a fine, sad, and wonderfully encouraging book.

It seems clear to me that the main obstacle to peace is *not* the atom bomb.

When I last talked to the great atomic physicist Niels Bohr – I think it was in 1952 – he said that the atom bomb would certainly preserve the peace. I was and am not so optimistic. But after all, he has been right up to now.

I see only one very difficult road to peace. It is a long road. Perhaps there will be a nuclear war long before we have taken a step along this road. Intellectuals, who mostly have the best of intentions, must first be persuaded to be a little more modest and not to try to play a leading role. No new ideologies, no new religion. Instead: 'A little more intellectual modesty.'[3]

We intellectuals know nothing. We grope our way along. Those of us who are scientists ought to be a little more modest and, above all, less dogmatic. Otherwise science will fall by the wayside – science, which is one of man's greatest and most promising creations.

Intellectuals know nothing. And their lack of modesty, their presumptuousness, is perhaps the greatest obstacle to peace on earth. The greatest hope is that, although they are arrogant, they may not be too stupid to realize it.

We will go on making mistakes. But there is hope that the following hypothesis may be true: without ideology, no war. The struggle against ideologies is in any case a struggle worth conducting.

I should like to finish by asking you once more not to believe anything that I have said, and to realize that I have no wish at all to end with a fanfare.

I only wanted to point out to you the great dangers lurking in ideologies, and to draw your attention to the dangerous need for knowledge, belief, and mutual suggestion that seems to lie hidden in our evolutionary biology and the structure of knowledge, as well as in our language.

Notes

1 'The Sun's singing, as of old, rivals the music of his brother spheres, and with thunderous course he completes his predestined circuit. The sight of him gives strength to the angels, though none of them can fathom his nature; the inconceivably lofty works of Creation are as splendid as on the first day.' *Faust Part One*, lines 243-250, plain prose translation from *Goethe: Selected Verse*, Penguin Classics, Harmondsworth, 1964, p. 180.

   Commentary:
   (1–2) The ancient harmony of the spheres.
   (3) Newton? No: Ptolemy.
   (4) *Sonnen-Untergang* [sun*set*] (Mozart, *Dies Irae*, or *Don Giovanni*).
   (6) In my edition there is a semi-colon at the end of this line. But I think it should be a colon: *'ergründen mag'* ['can fathom'] alludes to *'unbegreiflich'* [inconceivably'].
   (7–8) Men are among these works. They can grow in the Sun's thunderous course.

2 I owe the German expression *Suggestionsbedürfnis* to Professor E.K. Herz. This term cannot easily be translated into English.

3 I used the remark in inverted commas to sum up my criticism of Ernst Bloch in a television debate that I had with him in Vienna in 1968. Wolfgang Kraus was the presenter.

4

THE
EPISTEMOLOGICAL POSITION
OF
EVOLUTIONARY
EPISTEMOLOGY*

A priori – A posteriori

I should like to start by saying something about apriorism. First, I do not want anyone to tell me what terminology I should use. The main thing is that the terminology is clear. And the term 'genetically a priori' is completely clear, in my view at least. It means that something already exists *before* the a posteriori, *before* any perception. Besides, it is necessary to keep using the term 'a priori' because precisely here there is a quite definite relation to Kantianism. In my opinion, Kant becomes much more intelligible if one is clear that, very often at least, he meant 'genetically a priori', although of course he always spoke of 'a priori valid'.

Second, I should like to say that my view of Kant's a priori is completely different from the view developed by Konrad Lorenz many years ago. I have often spoken of this with Konrad Lorenz; but I am not exactly sure what his current view is. At the time when he wrote about Kantianism and published his interpretation, he thought that our remote ancestors got to know things through perception and that these things were then somehow taken from perception into the genetic structure; they thus became a priori for us, genetically a priori. My own view is completely different: that is, my theory, not my use of the concepts, is different. And theories are a hundred times more

* A spontaneous contribution to discussion at a symposium in Vienna, April 1986. First published in *Die Evolutionäre Erkenntnistheorie*, ed. by Rupert Riedl and Franz M. Wuketits, P. Parey, Berlin/Hamburg, 1987.

important than concepts. (Theories may be true or false. Concepts can at best be adequate and at worst be misleading. Concepts are unimportant, in comparison with theories.)

I should claim, then, that everything we know is genetically a priori. All that is a posteriori is the *selection* from what we ourselves have invented a priori.

In common with all other organisms that have something like perceptions and can use them to learn something, we must first, *before* we can do that (hence genetically a priori), have the ability to organize and interpret our sense impressions. But this is equivalent to Kantian a priori knowledge, as we can see especially clearly if we think of Kant's theory of space and time.

To say, as Konrad Lorenz does, that Kantian, innate, a priori knowledge was originally perceptual knowledge that we are now born with, because it has been inherited from our ancestors – is to ignore Kant's hugely important fundamental insight that perceptual knowledge is impossible without a priori knowledge. In reality, we should not even *attempt* to explain Kantian a priori knowledge in terms of perceptual knowledge. It was Kant's most significant achievement to show that all perceptual knowledge presupposes a priori knowledge.

Kant was the first to think that the existence of a priori knowledge is a necessary precondition for the existence of a posteriori knowledge. But from the 'necessity' of a priori knowledge for perceptual knowledge, we cannot infer 'necessity' in the sense of a logical modality. It is precisely here that I distance myself from Kant. As our perceptual knowledge is hypothetical, our a priori knowledge may also be hypothetical. And so it is in fact. Let us clarify this with an important example. In order to interpret what we perceive, we need a geometry that is *at least approximately* Euclidean – *at least* for our close surroundings. But it is another question whether the space that stretches beyond the earth and the moon is Euclidean or not. Here we come to hypotheses, to conjectural knowledge. Kant's view that all a priori knowledge is 'necessary', in the sense of 'not hypothetical but apodeictic', seems to me quite understandable but nevertheless unfounded and even mistaken.

For these and other reasons I assume, in sharp contrast to Kant, that our a priori knowledge – in geometry, for instance – has a hypothetical (or conjectural) character. I assume that it is only genetically a priori and *not valid a priori; not a priori necessary, not apodeictic.*

But even when this correction is made, Kant's apriorism is still of the greatest significance. And I would like to say clearly and explicitly that I am a radical apriorist (in the sense of the genetically a priori), much more radical than Kant, although my apriorism is a hypothetical or conjectural apriorism.

In the sharpest contrast to all epistemologists since John Locke, in contrast even to Kant, I support the thesis that all knowledge is a priori, genetically a priori, in its content. For all knowledge is hypothetical or conjectural: it is *our* hypothesis. Only the *elimination* of hypotheses is a posteriori, the clash between hypotheses and reality. In this alone consists the empirical component of our knowledge. And it is enough to enable us to learn from experience; enough for us to be empiricists.

To put this in another way: we learn *only* through trial and error. Our trials, however, are *always* our hypotheses. They stem from us, not from the external world. *All* we learn from the external world is that some of our efforts are mistaken.

From primitive forms of life onwards, from the earliest cells, adaptation is an invention on the part of living creatures. Living creatures adapt and themselves improve their adaptation. This theory of mine certainly leads to great difficulties. These difficulties are not present because my theory is difficult, but because we know so little. Of the origins of life and the earliest forms of adaptation, we know next to nothing. I will say something about this a little later.

Darwinism

I have made a very modest reformulation of Darwinism, of Darwin's theory of adaptation through selection. His theory states that *better-adapted individuals have a greater chance of having offspring.*

The theory, about whose history I could say quite a lot, may be found in this form in Darwin himself, and in my view it is a much clearer and better formulation than when people talk of 'natural selection' or 'the struggle for existence' and such things.

'Struggle for existence' and 'natural selection' are nothing but metaphors; they are not theories. For none of that exists at all. What exist are individuals who leave offspring behind them, and here it is precisely Darwin's theory that better-adapted individuals have a greater chance of leaving offspring. In this formulation, however, the limits of Darwinism are also plainly visible. For Darwinism has to assume that there are adapted, 'to some degree' adapted, individuals. And that takes us at once to the problem of the origins of life, about which we unfortunately still know very little indeed.

Adaptation and Darwinism:
A Thought Experiment

A thought experiment: I assume that we are able to produce life in a test tube (and I mean a test tube not a big machine). This does not seem so extraordinarily impossible, as we already know approximately how things fit together. And if we do not know it, we will perhaps in another hundred or thousand years.

We have produced life in a test tube, then, in the form of one or several genes. I assume we have a fairly simple gene, which duplicates itself there. This is a thought experiment involving the artificial emergence of life out of non-living ingredients. I know it is very improbable and very difficult, and Monod has made a rough estimate of this improbability. But let us assume we can do it. Then it is incredibly unlikely that this life we have produced will survive, *because there is no reason to assume that the life we have produced is adapted to a test tube*.

A test tube is a very poor environment for life, and to keep life alive we shall have to develop special machinery. We shall thus have to *adapt the environment to life*. (Adaptation is indeed based upon reciprocity.) To adapt the environment to life, we must introduce at least one supermarket to feed the life. We also need a sewage system to remove the waste produced by life. And then we must also build schools to get the children out of the way, which is the only purpose of schools. And we must organize birth control – otherwise the life we have made in the test tube will be choked by its descendants.

Now, the point of my thought experiment is twofold. First, I want to show that the mere coming into being of life does not solve any problems at all. Why is this newly emerged life adapted to its environment? I suspect that life had to emerge millions of times before it found an environment to which it was adapted. That it originated from some unknown chemical state does not at all mean that it arose in an environment where it could survive.

The improbability of such a coincidence of life with a potential (and thus adapted) environment is surely as great as the improbability of the emergence of life itself. As far as I am aware, this point has not been discussed before. I raise it here in connection with the problem of knowledge.

For the adaptation of life to its environment is a kind of knowledge. Without this minimal knowledge, life cannot survive. It is a knowledge of very *general* conditions of life. Either the conditions of which I have spoken (that is, the environment) must be adapted to life, or life must be adapted to the environment. It is, of course, based upon reciprocity.

If the environment is not reasonably stable – that is, if the conditions for adaptation are not constant over periods of time – we can be fairly sure that life will perish in an ecological catastrophe. By an ecological catastrophe I mean a change in those aspects of the environment that are adapted to life. If the environment changes in its suitability for life, life dies away: a catastrophe will have taken place, and the whole thing must start all over again. Thus, if the ecological conditions are not reasonably stable, we may assume that they were not good enough to keep life alive. History has to start again.

There must be some environmental stability, then, for there to be adaptation – or for there to be knowledge. Right from the start, a priori, life must know roughly as much about the environment as we had to know in our thought experiment about the life we produced and what it needed to survive. Adaptation is a form of a priori knowledge.

I have said all this not so much for the sake of the thought experiment as for the role that a priori knowledge plays in what others have called my 'evolutionary epistemology'. I have pointed out before that I did not apply this term to my theory of knowledge; it was others who described my theory of knowledge as evolutionary. Anyway, it is quite different from other evolutionary theories of knowledge.

I start from the assumption that life, from its very beginning, must have an innate anticipation of constant environmental conditions for life. It cannot be only *momentarily* adapted to these environmental conditions; it must be adapted to them *over periods of time*. And presumably this means that the environmental conditions must be fairly stable. It is true that life could from the start have been involved in anticipating all possible environmental changes, but that is really too implausible.

So we reach the conclusion that life must from the start anticipate in some degree the future of the environment: that is, all future states of the environment. Perhaps it is just a question of hours, or perhaps of millions of years. Life must be adapted to the future conditions of the environment; *and in this sense general knowledge comes earlier than momentary knowledge*, than special knowledge. Right from the start, life must be in this way equipped with general knowledge, with the knowledge we usually call knowledge of the laws of nature. Of course, this is not knowledge in the sense of conscious knowledge. Consciousness is quite another matter. So I have come to attribute knowledge to primeval life – which is obviously an *anthropomorphic idea*.

Let us now look at this anthropomorphism.

Homology, Knowledge, and Adaptation

I think it is foolish to do away with all anthropomorphism in biology. In this as in other areas we should adopt an evolutionary approach, and that means we should be thinking in terms of *homologies*.

When I treat my own nose and a dog's nose as homologous, this is the first step towards the theory of evolution. It is not at all self-evident that the dog has a nose; this is a theory of ours, and certainly a theory that a primeval man put forward. He treated his own nose and a dog's nose as homologous; and he would also have noticed that whereas dogs and some monkeys have tails, he does not have one himself. Such thinking in homologies is a *premise* of evolutionary thinking. And whenever one thinks in evolutionary terms, one has to accept such homologies – between our arms and the wings of birds, our legs and the legs of birds, our nose and the dog's nose. These are hypotheses of evolutionary theory: our nose and the dog's nose are evolutionarily homologous.

Such thinking in terms of homologies must be extended to our knowledge, to the acquisition of knowledge and to knowledge in general. Somehow or other, dogs and apes have something corresponding to our human knowledge. In fact, this is one reason why dogmatic behaviourism is, to be blunt, rather lacking in intelligence. It does not see that even if it only speaks of behaviour, it introduces a homology between our own behaviour and that of animals, and that this already entitles us to take such hypotheses about homology a little further.

Now, my fundamental epistemological thesis is that knowledge is of a high degree of generality and therefore *anticipatory*; it anticipates how the environment will be over a long period of time: for example, knowledge about the alternation of day and night that we *homologously* discover in flowers. (Flowers close up, etc.) Thus flowers 'know' something about general regularities. This does not mean they have understanding, only that they are suitably adapted. Obviously this happens through the expansion and contraction of tissues. But the tissues are so constructed that they are adapted to it; they presuppose the regularity.

My own position in epistemology goes further than that of all other epistemologists, whether evolutionary, Kantian, or non-evolutionary.

General adaptations precede momentary adaptations. They exist first. They are a priori.

Expectation

Before I take an example, I should like to introduce one more term. These forms of knowledge, or these adaptations, especially among animals, may be described as *expectations*.

The dog expects its master at half past five. It becomes restless, and one can see it is preparing for its master to come home at half past five. These are forms of knowledge, and these forms of knowledge are in every respect *expectations*. Similarly, flowers *expect* it to get colder in the evening; they prepare for it.

I would say that we (or those of us who are not blind) have eyes before we have perceptions with our eyes. And the fact that eyes are expectations – a form of inbuilt knowledge, and hence adaptation, in the eyes – can be clearly seen from the case of the Mexican axolotl. For in the Mexican axolotl, which grows up in caves, the eyes are completely atrophied. The Mexican axolotl is genetically blind. Every expectation that led to the evolution of our eyes is missing in its case; its eyes no longer play any role.

The eyes, then, are the expectation that we live in a world where there is at least sometimes light, and that they will then be able to use this light. This is the expectation that comes with the eyes we are born with. From an evolutionary standpoint, the eye exists before any perception of a face. And the eye, in other ways like perception of a face, is a kind of biological knowledge, for it is an anticipation or expectation.

As far as I am aware, virtually all epistemologists (as well as Konrad Lorenz, whom I admire enormously) start from the assumption that my knowledge is a result of my perception. Having revised this view, I see things quite differently. Perceptions are relatively unimportant paths to knowledge; what counts most is not that control of the momentary surroundings that allows us to have perceptions. Knowledge, fundamental knowledge, is rather like a feeler that we put out in all directions. The key thing, when I am here, is that I know I am in Vienna, I am in Austria. That kind of knowledge is more important for me than momentary perceptions, because it is fundamental to their interpretation.

Let us assume my view of evolutionary epistemology and start from completely general knowledge, coming then to certain special things such as the fact that I see some people I know over there. In this hall I can make out my friends among a crowd of unfamiliar faces; this is a function of momentary perception, for me at this particular moment. But the function is also, for me at this moment, less important than my general orientation, which leads me to what I have just been doing and what I have just been saying. And in this knowledge, this perceptual knowledge, we can and do repeatedly go astray.

Our perceptual knowledge is guided not only by what is anatomically and physiologically innate in us, the way in which our brains filter and, so to say, integrate everything. It is guided above all by our goals and intentions.

Let me tell a little story here.

Many, many years ago, it must be about sixty-five years ago, I was in the Dachstein mountains and wanted to go across from Karls-Eisfeld through a wind-gap. Then a mist came up, and I was looking in thick mist for a wind-gap when I finally saw something like it in the mist and ice. Naturally I thought I had found the wind-gap for which I had been looking for so long. But when I drew closer it was a large rock on the ice-field, and the rock had made the ice sink and form a trough. I had wrongly interpreted this as the sought-after wind-gap.

I am telling you this because it shows that our perceptions are partly dominated by our momentary expectations and interests. We are constantly active, as you can see in this case. I really do not see how one can speak of the perception of shapes and so on, as if my perception were rather like a photograph. I am active and seek things out and, in doing so, I interpret them in certain ways, sometimes completely in accordance with the aims or desires I am pursuing at the time. But these desires usually last quite a long time. I spent more than an hour looking for that wind-gap, which I did find in the end – and which looked quite different from what I had expected. Thus our goals, desires, and preferences play a huge role in life and in perception. They determine our interpretations, and we then try to test, to verify or falsify our interpretations.

There is something else I should like to say. The problem of reality has been discussed here. But I see this problem also in a different way. Reality is problematic for all of us. And we all continuously send out signals to be sure that we are not dreaming and that we live in a real world. We are like bats: although we do not quite have the technology of bats, we do have something similar. For example, I constantly change my position: it is one of my various techniques of signal transmission, and from the momentary return signals that I *actively* integrate, I learn that I am not dreaming and that reality does indeed make this strange impression.

I would argue, then, that living things are *active*: they are always casting about in every direction, like beetles. We feel our way towards things, with every means at our disposal. As long as we are not blind, our eyes are of the greatest importance. If we are blind but not also hard of hearing, our ears take over. And we can always use our fingers to try to grope our way along.

To my horror I have noticed (for it is an allegory I use from time to time) that my listeners see it as a kind of joke, but it is meant completely seriously. Our situation is always that of a black man looking in a black cellar for a black hat that may or may not be there. That is our situation – quite seriously. We are always know-nothings and always trying to find our way with our hands or our feet or our ears or our eyes, with any sense organs we have, which we use actively to make sure of the reality around us.

My theory of knowledge is thus quite revolutionary: it overturns everything my predecessors have said up to now. *We are active, we are constantly testing things out, constantly working with the method of trial and error.*

And that is the only method we have – also the only method we can assume the earliest animals or plants to have had. They move hither and thither, as Konrad Lorenz has so eloquently described it in more than one of his works. Primitive animals make trial movements, and somehow try to optimize something. Probably these trial movements are a question of instinctive weighing up. But perhaps they are not a question of anything mental at all, only of what is best for the mechanism they represent. They seek and they find; primitive animals are already looking for better surroundings, for a better world. And they are active in this quest for a better world. In this quest they must, as I said, already be somehow adapted: they must already have some general knowledge. Then come mutations and further adaptations. That is the empirical method: trial and error.

The empirical method is that which says 'no'. Unsuccessful trials, or mistakes, are eliminated. And this elimination leads in one way or another to fresh trials. Mutations and other means of changing DNA (to change heredity) play a major role in this.

The same results as those produced genetically can also be produced by traditional means. Lorenz claimed that something that is genetic in the grey goose (namely, the recognition of an enemy) is traditional in the jackdaw. His contrast between the two is especially beautifully drawn.

To sum up: from a biological point of view, animal and human knowledge consists in often unconscious expectations (or potential expectations).

Refutation of Induction

Life may thus, by very different means, take measures that are functionally similar but not genetically homologous. From this point of view, I should argue that there is no such thing as induction. I fear that hardly anyone agrees with me on this. But to me it seems a very trivial assertion! The idea of induction is an answer to the question: 'How do we know something?' – 'How do we arrive at our knowledge?'

The traditional answer is: 'Well, I open my eyes and look around; then I know.'

This way of justifying our knowledge may be found among nearly all epistemologists. Rudolf Carnap, for instance, writes: 'How do you know? Which are the perceptions which led to your opinion?'

For Carnap the second question is another way of putting the first.

It is taken for granted that I have perceptions and that these perceptions are the origin of my knowledge.

But I would argue that our knowledge is 99 per cent, or let us say 99.9 per cent, biologically innate. The rest is a modification, a revolutionary overturning of some previous knowledge, just as that knowledge was itself once a revolutionary overturning of something that went before. But in the end all knowledge goes back to innate knowledge and to its modification.

Innate knowledge but *not certain* knowledge. There is no certain knowledge. I cannot know, without constantly testing whether I am dreaming or not. We must constantly make sure of reality, by carrying out all possible checks. All that exists is conjectural knowledge.

I am sorry that Kant, whom I greatly like and admire, got this wrong, as have all other or almost all other philosophers. We are animals. We humans are animals, and animals cannot have certain knowledge. The Greeks already knew this. They said: 'The gods have certain knowledge – *epistēme*; men have only opinion – *doxa*.' Aristotle was the first to undo this correct and healthy insight. He said that we too have *epistēme* or certain, verifiable knowledge. And he came up with induction as a way to verifiable knowledge. But as he felt very uneasy about this, he made Socrates take the blame!

This cannot be discussed any further in the present context.

Kant was right that induction requires something prior to it, something universal. But this universal something, although a priori in preceding everything empirical (here Kant was right), was *not certain*. There is no certain knowledge. The word 'knowledge' [*Wissen*], at least in English and German, is the expression of a pipe-dream. The precise semantics of the word 'knowledge' is that knowledge is *certain* knowledge. I cannot say: 'I *know* I'm in Vienna, but I conjecture that I am.' You cannot say that: it would be to descend from knowledge to conjecture. If I say: 'I know I'm in Vienna', I must be *sure* that I'm in Vienna. But I am never completely sure of being in Vienna; I might possibly be having a very vivid dream. This is something, a possibility, that here and now plays a role in my life: namely, perhaps I am dreaming. It would be a very vivid dream, but as I am extremely tired, it would not be all that amazing.

In English and German 'knowledge' means *certain* knowledge. But there is no such thing. What we have at best is conjectural knowledge: that is all we can have. Our best knowledge, by far our best, is scientific knowledge. Yet scientific knowledge too is only conjectural knowledge.

Goals, Problems, Values

I am a little critical of a remark that my friend Riedl made in his introduction. He somehow joined forces – at least a little – with those who are dissatisfied with our reason. And he spoke in favour of cultural relativism. What I have to say will be quite different.

The task of us all as thinking human beings is to discover the truth. The truth is absolute and objective, but we do not have it in the bag. We are constantly seeking it and often find it only with difficulty; and we keep trying to improve our approximation to the truth. If truth were not absolute and objective, we should not be able to go wrong. Or our mistakes would be as good as our truth.

Our quest for the truth always proceeds as follows. *We invent* – a priori – our theories, our generalizations, including our gestalt perceptions. A gestalt perception is a hypothesis: it is our interpretation of what we see; and as an interpretation, the gestalt perception is a hypothesis. In general, we deal only with conjectures or (what is the same thing) with hypotheses. All the time we have conjectures made by ourselves. We keep trying somehow to compare these conjectures with reality, and in this way to improve them and bring them closer to reality.

I should be happy if scientists, and intellectuals in general, realized how little we know – for example, about the origins of life. We know next to nothing about it. These are the unsolved problems I have mentioned. Even if life emerges, why should it do so in just such a way that it happens to be adapted to the environment in which it has arisen? This is an extremely difficult problem.

We know nothing – that is the first point.

Therefore we should be very modest – that is the second.

That we should not claim to know when we do not know – that is the third.

This is more or less the approach I should like to popularize. It does not have good prospects.

5

TOWARDS AN
EVOLUTIONARY THEORY
OF KNOWLEDGE*

My dear Director, Ladies and Gentlemen,

In 1944 I was travelling with my wife in a bitterly cold bus, returning from a skiing holiday on Mount Cook. The bus stopped in the middle of nowhere, at a snowed-in rural New Zealand post office. To my surprise, I heard my name called, and someone handed me a telegram – the telegram that changed our lives. It was signed F.A. Hayek, and it offered me a Readership at the London School of Economics. The appointment followed in 1945, and in 1949 I was given the title of Professor of Logic and Scientific Method.

Today's lecture to the Alumni of the School, for which you, Dr Patel, so kindly invited me, is the first public lecture I have ever been asked to give at the L.S.E. I hope, Dr Patel, that you will allow me to regard it, quite informally, as my slightly belated Inaugural Address. It is an occasion to which I have been looking forward eagerly for the last 40 years.

My second request to you, dear Dr Patel, is to allow me to change the wording of the title of this address. When I was urged by the School to produce a title, I had little time to think. I now feel that 'Evolutionary Epistemology' sounds pretentious, especially since there exists a less pretentious equivalent. So, please let me change my title to its equivalent and let me call this Inaugural Address 'Towards an Evolutionary Theory of Knowledge'.

It is my aim, and my problem, at this Inaugural to interest you in work done and, even more, in work yet to be done in the theory of

* Lecture delivered at the London School of Economics, 9 June 1989, before the Alumni of the School; the Director of the School, Dr I. Patel, was in the chair. Published previously by Thoemmes Press, Bristol, as part of A *World of Propensities*, and reproduced here with kind permission.

knowledge, by placing it in the wide and exciting context of biological evolution, and to show you that we can learn something new from such an exercise.

I do not start by asking a question such as 'What is knowledge?' and, even less, 'What does "knowledge" mean?'. Instead, my starting point is a very simple proposition – indeed, an almost trivial one – the proposition *that animals can know something: that they can have knowledge.* For example, a dog may know that his master returns home, on working days, at about 6 p.m., and the behaviour of the dog may give many indications, clear to his friends, that he expects the return of his master at that time. I shall show that, in spite of its triviality, the proposition that *animals can know something* completely revolutionizes the theory of knowledge as it is still widely taught.

There are, of course, some people who would deny my trivial proposition. They might say, perhaps, that in attributing knowledge to the dog I am merely using a metaphor, and a blatant anthropomorphism. Even biologists interested in the theory of evolution have said such things. My reply is: yes, it is a blatant anthropomorphism, but it is not merely a metaphor. And the anthropomorphism is a very useful one: one that is indispensable in any theory of evolution. If you speak of the nose of the dog, or of his legs, then these are also anthropomorphisms, even though we take for granted that it is simply true that the dog has a nose – if somewhat different from our human nose.

Now, if you are interested in the theory of evolution, you will find that part of it is the important theory of homology, and that the dog's nose and my nose are homologous, which means that they are both inherited from a distant common ancestor. Without this hypothetical theory of homology, evolutionary theory could not exist. Obviously, the theory of homology is a highly speculative and very successful hypothesis, and one that all evolutionists adopt. My attribution of knowledge to the dog is therefore an anthropomorphism, but it is not just a metaphor. Rather, it implies the hypothesis that some organ of the dog, in this case presumably the brain, has a function that corresponds not only in some vague sense to the biological function of human knowledge, but is homologous with it.

Please note that the things that may be homologous are, in the original sense, organs. But they may also be functions of organs. And they may also be procedures. Even behaviour may be hypothesized to be homologous in the evolutionary sense; for example, courtship behaviour, especially ritualized courtship behaviour. That this is indeed homologous in the hereditary or genetic sense between, say, different but closely related species of birds, is very convincing. That it is homologous between ourselves and some species of fish seems highly dubious, yet it remains a serious hypothesis. Of course, the possession of a mouth or of a brain in fish is most convincingly homologous with our possession of the corresponding organs: it is quite convincing that they are genetically derived from the organs of a common ancestor.

I hope the central importance of the theory of homology for the theory of evolution has become sufficiently clear for my purpose; that is, for defending the existence of animal knowledge, not as a mere metaphor, but as a serious evolutionary hypothesis.

This hypothesis does in no way imply that animals will be aware of their knowledge; and it thereby draws attention to the fact that we ourselves possess knowledge of which we are not aware, not conscious.

Our own unconscious knowledge has often the character of unconscious *expectations*, and sometimes we may become conscious of having had an expectation of this kind when it turns out to have been mistaken.

An example of this is an experience that I had several times in my long career: in going down some stairs and reaching the last step, I almost fell, and became aware of the fact that I had unconsciously expected that there was one more step, or one fewer step, than actually existed.

This led me to the following formulation: when we are surprised by some happening, the surprise is usually due to an unconscious *expectation* that something else would happen.

I shall now try to give you a list of 19 interesting conclusions that we can draw, and partly have drawn (although so far unconsciously) from our trivial proposition that animals can know something.

1 Knowledge has often the character of expectations.
2 Expectations have usually the character of hypotheses, of conjectural or hypothetical knowledge: they are *uncertain*. And those who expect, or who know, may be quite unaware of this uncertainty. In the example of the dog, the dog may die without ever having been disappointed in this expectation of his master's timely return: but *we* know that the timely return was never certain, and that the dog's expectation was a very risky hypothesis. (After all, there might have been a railway strike.) So we can say:
3 Most kinds of knowledge, whether of men or animals, are hypothetical or conjectural; especially the very ordinary kind of

knowledge, just described as having the character of an expectation; say, the expectation, supported by a printed official timetable, that at 5.48 p.m. there will arrive a train from London. (In some libraries, embittered or merely discerning readers returned timetables to the shelves headed 'Fiction'.)

4   In spite of its uncertainty, of its hypothetical character, much of our knowledge will be objectively *true*: it will correspond to the objective *facts*. Otherwise we could hardly have survived as a species.

5   We therefore must clearly *distinguish* between the *truth* of an expectation or a hypothesis and its *certainty*; and therefore between two ideas: *the idea of truth* and *the idea of certainty*; or, as we may also say, between *truth* and *certain truth* – for example, a mathematically demonstrable truth.

6   There is much truth in much of our knowledge, but little certainty. We must approach our hypotheses *critically*; we must test them as severely as we can, in order to find out whether they cannot be shown to be false after all.

7   Truth is objective: it is correspondence to the facts.

8   Certainty is rarely objective: it is usually no more than a strong feeling of trust, of conviction, although based on insufficient knowledge. Such feelings are dangerous since they are seldom well-founded. Strong feelings of conviction make dogmatists of us. They may even turn us into hysterical fanatics who try to convince themselves of a certainty which they unconsciously know is not available.

Before proceeding with this list to the next point (to point 9), I wish to digress for a moment. For I want to say a few words against the widespread doctrine of sociological relativism, often unconsciously held, especially by sociologists who study the ways of scientists and who think that they thereby study science and scientific knowledge. Many of these sociologists do not believe in objective truth, but think of truth as a sociological concept. Even a former scientist such as the late Michael Polanyi thought that truth was what the experts *believe* to be true – or, at least, the great majority of the experts. But in all sciences, the experts are sometimes mistaken. Whenever there is a breakthrough, a really important new discovery, this means that the experts have been proved wrong, and that the facts, the objective facts, were different from what the experts expected them to be. (Admittedly, a breakthrough is not a frequent event.)

I do not know of any creative scientist who has made no mistakes;

and here I am thinking of the very greatest – Galileo, Kepler, Newton, Einstein, Darwin, Mendel, Pasteur, Koch, Crick, and even Hilbert and Gödel. Not only are all animals fallible, but also all men. So there are experts, but no authorities – a fact that has not yet established itself sufficiently. Of course, we are all very conscious of the fact that we ought not to make mistakes, and we all try very hard. (Perhaps Gödel tried harder than anyone else.) But still, we are fallible animals – fallible mortals, as the early Greek philosophers would have it: only the Gods can know, we mortals can only opine and guess.

I guess, indeed, that it is the suppressed sense of our own fallibility that is responsible for our despicable tendency to form cliques and to go along with whatever seems to be fashionable: that makes so many of us howl with the wolves. All this is human weakness, which means it ought not to exist. But it does exist, of course; it is even to be found among some scientists. And as it exists, we ought to combat it; first in ourselves, and then, perhaps, in others. For I hold that science *ought* to strive for objective truth, for truth that depends only on the facts; on truth that is above human authority and above arbitration, and certainly above scientific fashions. Some sociologists fail to understand that this objectivity is a possibility towards which science (and therefore scientists) should aim. Yet science *has* aimed at truth for at least 2,500 years.

But let us now return to our evolutionary theory of knowledge, to our trivial starting proposition that animals can know something, and to our list of results obtained from, or suggested by, this trivial proposition.

9 Can only animals know? Why not plants? Obviously, in the biological and evolutionary sense in which I speak of knowledge, not only animals and men have expectations and therefore (unconscious) knowledge, but also plants; and, indeed, all organisms.

10 Trees know that they may find much-needed water by pushing their roots into deeper layers of the earth; and they know (or the tall ones do) how to grow up vertically. Flowering plants know that warmer days are about to arrive, and they know how and when to open their flowers, and to close them – according to sensed changes in radiation intensity or in temperature. Thus they have something like sensations or perceptions to which they respond, and something like sense organs. And they know, for example, how to attract bees and other insects.

11 An apple tree that sheds its fruit or its leaves offers a beautiful

example for one of the central points of our investigations. The tree is adapted to the seasonal changes of the year. Its structure of inbuilt biochemical processes keeps them in step with these law-like and long-term environmental changes. It expects these changes: it is attuned to them, it has foreknowledge of them. (Trees, especially tall trees, are also finely adjusted to such invariants as gravitational forces.) But the tree responds, in an appropriate and well-adapted manner, also to short-term changes and forces, and even to momentary events in the environment. Chemical changes in the stems of the apples and of the leaves prepare them for falling; but they usually fall in response to the momentary pull of the wind: the ability to respond appropriately to short-term or even momentary events or changes in the environment is closely analogous to the ability of an animal to respond to short-term perceptions, to sense experiences.

12 The distinction between adaptation to, or (unconscious) knowledge of, law-like and long-term environmental conditions, such as gravity and the cycle of the changing seasons, on the one side, and adaptation to, or knowledge of, environmental short-term changes and events, on the other side, is of the greatest interest. While short-term events occur in the life of the individual organisms, the long-term and law-like environmental conditions are such that adaptation to them must have been at work throughout the evolution of countless generations. And if we look more closely at short-term adaptation, at the knowledge of, and the response to, environmental short-term events, then we see that the *ability* of the individual organism to respond appropriately to short-term events (such as a particular pull of the wind or, in the animal kingdom, the appearance of a foe) is also a long-term adaptation, and also the work of adaptation going on through countless generations.

13 A grazing flock of wild geese is approached by a fox. One of them sees the fox and gives the alarm. It is precisely a situation like this – a short-term event – in which the eyes of an animal can save its life. The animal's ability to respond appropriately depends on its possession of eyes – of sense organs – adapted to an environment in which daylight is periodically available (analogous to the change of the seasons or to the constant availability of the directional pull of gravity, used by the tree to find the direction of its growth); in which deadly foes are threatening (that is, in which crucially significant objects exist for visual identification);

and in which escape is possible if these foes are identified *at a sufficient distance.*

14 All this adaptation is of the nature of long-term knowledge about the environment. And a little thinking will make it clear that without this kind of adaptation, without this kind of knowledge of law-like regularities, sense organs like the eyes would be useless. Thus we must conclude that the eyes could never have evolved without an unconscious and very rich knowledge about long-term environmental conditions. This knowledge, no doubt, evolved together with the eyes and with their use. Yet at every step it must have somehow preceded the evolution of the sense organ, and of its use. For the knowledge of the pre-conditions of its use are built into the organ.

15 Philosophers and even scientists often assume that all our knowledge stems from our senses, the 'sense data' which our senses deliver to us. They believe (as did, for example, the famous theorist of knowledge, Rudolf Carnap) that the question 'How do you know?' is in every case equivalent to the question 'What are the *observations* that entitle you to your assertion?'. But seen from a biological point of view, this kind of approach is a colossal mistake. For our senses to tell us anything, we must have *prior* knowledge. In order to be able to see a thing, we must know what 'things' are: that they can be located within some space; that some of them can move while others cannot; that some of them are of immediate importance to us, and therefore are noticeable and will be noticed, while others, less important, will never penetrate into our consciousness: they may not even be unconsciously noticed, and they may simply leave no trace whatever upon our biological apparatus. For this apparatus is highly active and selective, and it actively selects only what is at the moment of biological importance. But in order to do so, it must be able to use adaptation, expectation: prior knowledge of the situation must be available, including its possibly significant elements. This prior knowledge cannot, in turn, be the result of observation; it must, rather, be the result of an evolution by trial and error. Thus the eye itself is not the result of observation, but the result of evolution by trial and error, of adaptation, of non-observational long-term knowledge. And it is the result of such knowledge, derived not from short-term observation, but from adaptation to the environment and to such situations as constitute the *problems to be solved in the task of living;* situations that make our organs, among them our sense organs, significant instruments in the moment-by-moment task of living.

16 I hope I have been able to give you some idea of the importance of the distinction between long-term and short-term adaptation, long-term and short-term knowledge, and of the fundamental character of long-term knowledge: of the fact that it must always precede short-term or observational knowledge, and of the impossibility that long-term knowledge can be obtained from short-term knowledge alone. Also, I hope that I have been able to show you that both kinds of knowledge are hypothetical: both are conjectural knowledge, although in a different way. (Our knowledge, or a tree's knowledge, of gravity will turn out to be gravely mistaken if we, or the tree, are placed in a no-longer accelerated rocket or ballistic missile.) Long-term conditions (and the knowledge of them) may be subject to revision; and an instance of short-term knowledge may turn out to be a misinterpretation.

And so we come to the decisive and perhaps most general proposition, valid for all organisms including man, even though it may perhaps not cover all forms of human knowledge.

17 All adaptations to environmental and to internal regularities, to long-term situations and to short-term situations, are kinds of knowledge – kinds of knowledge whose great importance we can learn from evolutionary biology. There are, perhaps, some forms of human knowledge that are not, or not obviously, forms of adaptations, or of attempted adaptations. But, roughly speaking, almost all forms of knowledge of an organism, from the unicellular amoeba to Albert Einstein, serve the organism to adapt itself to its actual tasks, or to tasks that may turn up in the future.

18 Life can only exist, and can only survive, if it is in some degree adapted to its environment. We can thus say that knowledge – primitive knowledge, of course – is as old as life. It originated together with the origin of pre-cellular life, more than three thousand eight hundred million years ago. (Unicellular life came into existence not much later.) This happened soon after the earth cooled down sufficiently to allow some of the water in its atmosphere to liquify. Until then, water had existed only in the form of steam or clouds, but now hot liquid water began to collect in rocky basins, big or small, forming the first rivers, lakes, and seas.

19 Thus, the origin and the evolution of knowledge may be said to coincide with the origin and the evolution of life, and to be closely linked with the origin and evolution of our planet earth. Evolutionary theory links knowledge, and with it ourselves, with

the cosmos; and so the problem of knowledge becomes a problem of cosmology.

Here I end my list of some of the conclusions that can be drawn from the proposition that animals can have knowledge.

I may perhaps very briefly refer to my book, *The Logic of Scientific Discovery*, first published in German in 1934, and published in English for the first time 25 years later, in 1959. In the Preface to the first English edition I wrote of the fascination of the *problem of cosmology*; and I said of it: 'It is the problem of understanding the world – including ourselves, and our knowledge, as part of the world.'

This is how I still see the setting of the evolutionary theory of knowledge.

When our solar system evolved and the earth had cooled sufficiently, there must have developed conditions in some place on earth that were favourable to the origin and to the evolution of life. Unicellular bacterial life quickly spread all over the earth. But those originally so very favourable local conditions could hardly have prevailed over many different geographical regions; so it seems that life must have had a struggle. Yet, in a comparatively short time, many different bacterial forms evolved that were adapted to very different environmental conditions.

Such, it appears, are the facts. Of course, they are far from certain: they are hypothetical interpretations of some geological findings. But if they are even approximately correct, they refute, for two reasons, the at present most widely accepted theory of the origin of life: the so-called 'soup theory' or 'broth theory'.

First reason: as the leading defenders of the soup theory assert, this theory demands a low temperature for the soup or broth in which the macromolecules develop, and later join up to form the first organism. The reason for their assertion is that, if the temperature is not very low (the broth must be considerably supercooled below 0°C), the macromolecules quickly decompose, instead of joining up.

But what we know of the earth in those days indicates that no such cool places existed. The surface of the earth, and even more the seas, were much hotter than today; and even today a watering place supercooled below 0°C would not easily be available, except perhaps near the North Pole or within a refrigerating plant.

Second reason: the theory that the macromolecules in the soup have joined up, and so have organized themselves into a living organism, is improbable in the extreme. The improbability is so great that one would have to assume an extremely long time-span in order to make the event a little less improbable; a time-span far longer, indeed, than the calculated time for which the cosmos has existed. So say even some of the most prominent defenders of the soup theory.

This constitutes a sound refutation of the theory in question, for as geologists found, the time-span between the formation of (boiling hot) liquid water and the origin of life is surprisingly short, and far too short to allow for an event of such extreme improbability to happen – even if the high temperature were acceptable to the soup theorists.

These two reasons constitute two refutations of the at present ruling soup theory of the origin of life. (There are many other refutations.) It is therefore fortunate that an alternative theory was published in 1988, a theory which is not beset by these or by similar difficulties. It assumes only the existence of such simple inorganic micromolecules as those of water, iron, carbon dioxide and hydrosulphide. No organic macromolecules are assumed to be present before the first metabolic cycles start and, with them, the chemical self-organizing of life. The new theory shows in detail how organic molecules (such as sugar) may evolve in time, perhaps deep down in the sea, bound to the surface of pyrite crystals, rather than in a solution. The anaerobic formation of the pyrite crystal creates the free chemical energy needed for the chemical processes – especially carbon fixation – that constitute the earliest form of pre-cellular life.

This new theory of the origin of life has been developed by its author in considerable detail, and it seems to be very successful: it explains many biochemical pathways. It is readily testable by experiments. But its greatest strength is that it can explain many biochemical facts that were unexplained before.

Günter Wächtershäuser, the author of this new biochemical theory, has also provided another biochemical theory – one that is of still greater relevance to the evolutionary theory of knowledge and to the problems we are discussing here. He has produced a biochemical theory of the origin of the first light-sensitive organ; that is, of the earliest evolutionary predecessor of our eyes. Since our eyes are our most important sense organs, this result is of great interest to our discussion.

The main result is this. It is known that some early unicellular micro-organism, presumably a bacterium, invented a revolutionary electro-chemical method of transforming sunlight into chemical energy: a method of using sunlight as a food, a method of feeding on sunlight. It was a bold and, indeed, a dangerous invention since, as we all know, too much sunlight – and especially the ultraviolet portion of sunlight – can kill. So with this invention, several problems arose for the cell (that previously may have been living deep down in the dark sea). They were pointed out by Wächtershäuser.

The first problem was to find out *where* sunlight is and, by using this information, to move towards it. This problem was solved by the first formation of a sense organ with the function of our eyes, a sense organ chemically linked to some already existing executive mechanism for the movement of the cell.

A second problem that arose was that of avoiding the danger of getting too much ultraviolet sunlight: of moving away in time, before suffering damage, towards some shade, presumably towards a deeper layer of sea water.

Thus in the evolution of the eye, even its earliest predecessor had to become a *controller of the movement of the cell*. It had to become part of the feeding mechanism of the cell, and part of its security movements: its mechanism for evading danger. The eye helped to avoid radiation damage to the cell – to anticipate danger. Even its very first function assumed prior knowledge of environmental states and possibilities.

Wächtershäuser pointed out that the revolutionary invention of feeding on sunlight would have been self-destructive without that other, that essentially protective invention of moving out of sunlight (and presumably also into it) becoming part of the invention of the early eye and its link to the apparatus of motion. And so the problem arises in his theory: how could these two great inventions come together?

If we take an interest in biological evolution, especially in early evolution, then we must be constantly aware of the fact that life is, basically, a chemical *process*. It was Heraclitus, half a millennium before the birth of Christ, who said that life was a process, like fire; and, indeed, our life is something like a complex process of chemical oxidation. In the earliest stages of its evolution, when free oxygen was not available, sulphur played its role instead. As you may know, it was the bacterial invention of using sunlight as food – which, incidentally, led later to the self-invention of the kingdom of plants – that produced the greatest of all life-induced revolutions in the history of our environment: it introduced oxygen into the atmosphere. And so it created the air that we know, that makes *our* life possible, life as we know it: *our* breathing, *our* lungs, *our* fire (within and without). Heraclitus was right: we are not things, but flames. Or a little more prosaically, we are, like all cells, *processes of metabolism*; nets of chemical processes, of highly active (energy-coupled) chemical pathways.

The great Belgian biochemist Marcel Florkin (1900–1979) was one of the first to see clearly that *the evolution of life, or organisms, is an evolution of nets of chemical pathways.* The net of pathways that constitutes a cell at some given period of time may make it possible for some *new* pathway, often just a slight variation, to graft itself upon the then extant system. The new pathway may have been impossible without some of the chemical compounds produced by the old system of pathways. As Florkin pointed out, the net of chemical pathways of an extant cell often still retains, as part of this net, the archaic pathways of some billion years ago that made the later graftings possible. This, as Florkin pointed out, is analogous to the way in which anatomic pathways of the anatomic construction of the developing embryo may still retain those of its archaic ancestors of, say, some hundred million years ago. Thus the extant pathways of the metabolism may reveal some of its evolutionary history; a situation analogous to the so-called 'biogenetic law' of Fritz Müller and Ernst Haeckel.

It is within this setting of Florkin's ideas that Wächtershäuser was able to explain the riddle of the coincidence of the two great inventions: the invention of feeding on sunlight and the invention of light-sensitivity, of the archaic eye. The explanation is that both inventions are chemically very closely related: one of the pathways producing the machinery for feeding on sunlight and the pathway for producing the visual apparatus are structurally connected.

We may speculate that the invention resulted from the general tendency of organisms to explore their environment; in this case, by rising towards the surface layer of the sea. Presumably, the one or the other of these bacteria had, accidentally, evolved to a stage that made it possible to invent both of these new, chemically connected, grafts. Other organisms will also have boldly ventured near the surface, only to be destroyed by sunlight. But one (or perhaps a few) had the right chemical outfit, and survived. It was able to turn the surface layer of the sea into the richest feeding ground for its offspring; and its offspring exuded those huge amounts of oxygen that transformed the atmosphere.

We see that the Darwinian trial-and-error method turns out to be a method of the (partly accidental) variation and accretion of chemical pathways. In extant cells the pathways are controlled, step by chemical step, by enzymes which are highly specific chemical catalysts, that is, chemical means of speeding up specific chemical steps; and the enzymes are partly controlled by the genes. But a genetic mutation, and the synthesis of a new enzyme, will not lead to a new step in the net of pathways unless the new enzyme accidentally fits into the extant net; it is always the existing structure of the net of pathways that determines what new variations or accretions are possible. It is the existing net that contains the potentiality for new inventions; and a fitting enzyme, if not yet available, may become available soon. In some cases it may decide the future evolution of the species by determining which of the potential steps will be realized. (One step may lead to a slow evolution while another step may lead to a cascade of further steps. Both steps will be equally Darwinian, since they are subject to selection; their apparently different speeds are likely to be explicable in chemical terms.)

I will now try to list some of the lessons to be learnt for the theory of knowledge from all that has been said so far.

The main lesson to be drawn may be formulated, perhaps with some little exaggeration, as follows. Even in the most primitive organisms, and even in the most primitive cases of sensitivity, everything depends upon the organism itself: upon its structure, its state, its activity. More especially, even if we confine our discussion for the moment to the problem of obtaining some knowledge from the environment with the help of the organism's sensitivity to the momentary state of its environment, even then everything will depend on the organism's own state, its long-term structure, its state of preparation for solving its problems, its state of activity.

In order to develop more fully what I have just said only very roughly, it is useful to introduce here a variant of the Kantian terminology of *a priori* and *a posteriori*. In Kant, knowledge *a priori* means knowledge that we possess *prior* to sense-observation; and knowledge *a posteriori* means knowledge we possess *posterior* to sense-observation, or after observation; and I will use the terms '*a priori*' and '*a posteriori*' only in this temporal or historical sense. (Kant himself uses his term *a priori* to mean, in addition, knowledge that is not merely prior to observation but also '*a priori* valid'; by which he means necessarily or certainly true. Of course, I shall not follow him in this since I am stressing the uncertain and conjectural character of our knowledge.) So I shall use the term '*a priori*' to characterize that kind of knowledge – of fallible or conjectural knowledge – which an organism has *prior to sense experience*; roughly speaking, it is *inborn* knowledge. And I shall use the term '*a posteriori*' for knowledge that is obtained with the help of the sensitivity of the organism to momentary changes in the state of its environment.

Using this Kantian terminology with the modifications I have just indicated, we can now say that Kant's own position – highly revolutionary at the time – is this.

(A) Most knowledge of detail, of the momentary state of our surroundings, is *a posteriori*.

(B) But such *a posteriori* knowledge is impossible without the *a priori* knowledge that we somehow *must* possess before we can acquire observational or *a posteriori* knowledge: without it, *what our senses tell us can make no sense.* We must first have established an overall frame of reference, or else there will be no context available to make sense of our sensations.

(C) This *a priori* knowledge contains, especially, knowledge of the structure of space and time (of space and time relations), and of causality (of causal relations).

I think that, in all these points, Kant is right. (Incidentally, I also think that he had hardly a real successor in this except perhaps Schopenhauer.) In my opinion, Kant anticipated the most important results of the evolutionary theory of knowledge.

But I am going much further than Kant. I think that, say, 99 per cent of the knowledge of all organisms is inborn and incorporated in our biochemical constitution. And I think that 99 per cent of the knowledge taken by Kant to be *a posteriori* and to be '*data*' that are 'given' to us through our senses is, in fact, not *a posteriori,* but *a priori.* For our senses can serve us (as Kant himself saw) only with yes-and-no answers to our own questions; questions that we conceive, and ask, *a priori;* and questions that sometimes are very elaborate. Moreover, even the yes-and-no answers of the senses have to be *interpreted* by us – interpreted in the light of our *a priori* preconceived ideas. And, of course, they are often *misinterpreted.*

Thus, all our knowledge is hypothetical. It is an adaptation to a partly unknown environment. It is often successful and often unsuccessful, the result of anticipatory trials and of unavoidable errors, *and of error elimination.* Some of the errors that have entered the inheritable constitution of an organism are eliminated by eliminating their bearer; that is, the individual organism. But some errors escape, and this is one reason why we are all fallible: our adaptation to the environment is never optimal, and it is always imperfect. A frog is constituted *a priori* so that it can see its prey – a fly – only when the fly moves. When the fly sits still, the frog cannot see it, even if it is very close: the frog's adaptation is imperfect.

Organisms and their organs incorporate expectations about their environment; and expectations – as we have seen – are homologous with our theories: as homologous as is the nose of my dog with my nose. So I suggest the hypothesis that adaptations and expectations are homologous even with *scientific theories* (and *vice versa* theories with adaptations and expectations). Theories may often contain evaluations. A unicellular organism's sensitivity to light, to heat, and to acidity may help it to escape from too little or too much of any of these. The organism's structure may incorporate the theory: 'the surrounding water can be dangerous: it may be too hot or too cold, and it may be too much or too little acid.' Clearly, such evaluations can evolve only if the organism is *able to take action*; for example, by moving away if it anticipates danger from these environmental states. Problems, values, and activity all evolve together.

I have said something about the origin of the archaic eye; and we can now say that its invention incorporates new discoveries, new theories, new knowledge about the environment and also the possibility of new values. For the first bacterium that not only achieved the new chemical synthesis, but went with it to a layer near the surface of the sea and survived, after millions of its brothers had succumbed, proved by its survival that it had solved a *problem* of adaptation; and in solving a *problem*, it introduced a new theory about new *values*. The invention was incorporated in the structure of the organism; in new, inheritable knowledge and therefore in new *a priori* knowledge.

Within this great revolution, the momentary signals conveyed by the eye to the organism were as such comparatively unimportant. They became important only together with the state of the organism; say, its need for food. The eye certainly helped the organism to feed on sunrays without destruction. But signals as such that, by homology, we might call the 'data' need not even be noticed. What leads to action are the *interpreted* signals (and interpretation is part of the action): signals *plus* the new theoretical evaluation of advantages and of danger; not objective 'data', but enticements and warnings acquired and *interpreted* with the help of the *a priori* structure of the organism.

We have seen that, even in bacteria, theories or hypotheses come before the signals, the 'sensations'. I need hardly stress that, especially in science, hypotheses come *before* what some scientists still call the 'data'; misleadingly, because they are not *given* to us, but actively (and sometimes at great peril) *sought and acquired* by us.

Observations (or 'data') may lead in science to the *abandonment* of a scientific theory and thereby induce some of us to think up a new tentative theory – a new trial. But the new theory is *our* product, *our* thought, *our* invention; and a new theory is only rarely thought up by more than a few people, even when there are many who agree on the refutation of the old theory. The few are those who *see the new problem*. Seeing a new problem may well be the most difficult step in creating a new theory.

The invention of the eye is thus an invention of new theoretical *a priori* knowledge, of an adaptation to the environment. It was from the first an adaptation to a long-term environmental structure: to the existence of potentially edible sunlight; it thus incorporates knowledge of this environmental structure. It is theoretical knowledge of a high degree of universality, almost like Kantian knowledge of space and time. It creates the possibility of momentary 'observation' or, more precisely, of the adaptation to a momentary situation of the environment. It may induce in the organism states of enticement or of repulsion, and it may make possible the release of prepared actions upon the environment. Thus, the invention of a highly universal theory (in this case the invention of a sense organ) may come before the observation (the use of the sense organ): it makes observation possible and introduces it into the set of actions that are available to the organism. And so it is itself an adaptation, found by trial and error. Theories (scientific or otherwise) are trials, inventions; they are *not* the results of many observations; they are *not* derived from many data.

Clearly, the first invention of the eye was a great achievement. Much of it has been preserved, and much evolved further. And yet, we – in common with all animals – have forgotten the knowledge that sunlight is edible, and how to eat it. And to this day we have not fully regained this knowledge.

Ladies and Gentlemen, I am one of those who love science and who think that science is enlightened common sense. I even think it is not much more than enlightened bacterial common sense! This is a view that, admittedly, clashes with common sense; but I hope that I have shown in this lecture that it need not clash with *enlightened* common sense. I have, I believe, refuted classical empiricism – the bucket theory of the mind that says that we obtain knowledge just by opening our eyes and letting the sense-given or god-given 'data' stream into a brain that will digest them.

Christopher Isherwood expressed this view by the title of his book, *I am a Camera.* But when he chose this title he forgot that even a camera must have an *a priori* built-in constitution; that there are primitive cameras and surprisingly evolved ones; and that in a failing light in which a bad camera records nothing, a good camera may produce a perfect picture, giving us all we want of it. It is better adapted to the environment, and also to our needs, that is, to our problems: it incorporates certain values that we have evolved while working on the evolution of the camera. But a lot of things it cannot do; for example, it cannot improve itself; and it cannot invent a new important problem, or a new tentative solution.

All organisms are problem finders and problem solvers. And all problem solving involves evaluations and, with these, values. Only with life do problems and values enter the world. And I do not believe that computers will ever invent important new problems, or new values.

Of these new values that we have invented, two seem to me the most important for the evolution of knowledge: a self-critical attitude – a value that we should always teach ourselves to live up to; and truth – a value that we should always seek our theories to live up to.

The first of these values, a self-critical attitude, first enters the world with certain objective products of life, such as spiders' webs, birds' nests, or beaver dams: products that can be repaired or improved. The emergence of the self-critical attitude is the beginning of something even more important: of *the critical approach,* an approach that is critical in the interest of *objective truth.* (I hope that it was the critical approach that inspired the Founders of the London School of Economics to choose the dam-repairing beaver for its coat of arms.)

Both of these values, the critical approach and objective truth, enter our world only with the human language, the first and most important product of the human mind. Language makes it possible to consider our theories critically: to look at them as if they were external objects, as if they belonged to the world outside of ourselves which we share with others. Theories become objects of criticism, like the beaver dam. And we can try to repair them in the light of that most important value: correspondence to the facts – *truth.*

I have often said that from the amoeba to Einstein there is only one step. Both work with the method of trial and error. The amoeba must hate error, for it dies when it errs. But Einstein knows that we can learn only from our mistakes, and he spares no effort to make new trials in order to detect new errors, and to eliminate them from our theories. The step that the amoeba cannot take, but Einstein can, is to achieve a critical, a self-critical attitude, a critical approach. It is the greatest of the virtues that the invention of the human language puts within our grasp. I believe that it will make peace possible.

Let me end with a quotation from Albrecht Dürer, an artist and a scientist:

> But I shall let the little I have learnt go forth into the day in order that someone better than I may guess the truth, and in his work may prove and rebuke my error. At this I shall rejoice that I was yet the means whereby this truth has come to light.

6

KEPLER'S METAPHYSICS OF THE SOLAR SYSTEM AND HIS EMPIRICAL CRITICISM*

Yesterday – eight days before the 356th anniversary of Kepler's death – marked another significant date in the story of Kepler. For 7 November 1631 was the day on which Pierre Gassendi observed and confirmed the passing of the planet Mercury in front of the sun, an event that Kepler had predicted two years before. Kepler was no longer able to witness this first empirical corroboration of his new theory of the planets. He had died the previous year, shortly before his fifty-ninth birthday.

First I must make it absolutely clear that I am no Kepler expert; I am no more than an enthusiastic admirer and follower. What fills me with enthusiasm is his glowing love and relentless quest for the truth, as we can see especially in his *Astronomia Nova*; but also the creative metaphysics that animates his whole work and reaches maturity in his magnificent *Harmonices Mundi* (Harmony of the World).

I want first to make a couple of brief observations. The first concerns Kepler's metaphysics and the sense in which I am a follower of it – only hypothetically, of course, only experimentally – and the second, my agreement with Kepler's method, in which his metaphysics plays such a major role.

Let me begin, then, with Kepler's metaphysics. Like all genuine scientists and seekers after truth, Kepler looks for the reality behind appearances: hypothetical reality is supposed to explain appearances. And like all seekers after truth, he makes many mistakes. But he learns from his mistakes, as few others have done.

---

* Revised form of a lecture given on 8 November 1986 in Linz. First published in *Wege der Vernunft. Festschrift zum siebzigsten Geburtstag von Hans Albert*, ed. by Alfred Bohnen and Alan Musgrave, J.C.B. Mohr/Paul Siebeck, Tübingen, 1991

The reality that Kepler seeks behind appearances is inspired by the Pythagoreans and his own interest in music. He thinks that the world is filled with melodious sound, conducted and held together by harmony and resonance, but also by dissonances and their eventual resolution. It is a divine symphony, an architecture of divine, heavenly beauty. This idea makes of him a relentless seeker after truth. The truth *must* be beautiful; it must reveal a reality of heavenly beauty. Kepler wanted to discover this reality – not only approximately but precisely, just as it really is.

This explains why he took so seriously even a slight deviation from a hypothetical orbit, a deviation of just eight minutes of arc, calculated from the observations of Tycho Brahe. On this deviation of eight minutes of arc discovered by Kepler everything else depends: Newton's dynamics and hence the whole of modern physics. For Kepler it was a dissonance that his love of truth and his metaphysics made impossible to bear: it had to be resolved. This required his metaphysics. And his resolution of the dissonance peaked in the *Harmonices Mundi*, his most mature metaphysics. Not only Newton's classical physics but also wave mechanics ultimately originated in the tension between those eight minutes of arc – less than one-seventh of one degree – and Kepler's Pythagorean metaphysics. Like the theory of atoms, which began in its Greek form as metaphysics in the fifth century B.C. (Leucippus and Democritus) and acquired scientific status only in the nineteenth and twentieth centuries A.D., Kepler's *Harmony of the World* acquired scientific status only with Louis de Broglie and Erwin Schrödinger. In fact, Schrödinger's wave mechanics takes the transition from geometric radial optics to wave optics and attempts to transpose it to the theory of matter, to the theory of elementary particles. Wave optics in turn takes its orientation from musical theory, from the theory of acoustic vibrations and waves, resonance and dissonance. But in this theory Kepler and his doctrine of harmony – hence Pythagoras in the end – plays a decisive role.[1]

Kepler, then, plays a role in the prehistory of Schrödinger's wave mechanics. But that is not all. Of all Schrödinger's precursors, Kepler is the only one who foresaw that harmony – resonance – holds the world together. For the most important consequence of Schrödinger's wave mechanics may well be that resonance holds together atoms and molecules, in particular the giant molecules of DNA.

As Einstein and de Broglie and his disciples already suspected, there probably is indeed something that may be described as empty, matter-free de Broglie waves. This seems to be confirmed by the results of the great Viennese experimental physicist Helmut Rauch, at least for neutron waves, which are most important for this problem. Here we have confirmation of what we have known since Newton's forces and Faraday's and Maxwell's fields: namely, that there are physically effective but immaterial (that is, matterless physical) structures that are in the closest interaction with matter.

I am opposed to Niels Bohr's famous theory of the complementarity of particles and waves, according to which an unknown 'thing in itself' appears now as particle, now as wave, but in such a way that these two forms of appearance exclude each other. (This theory is refuted by, among other effects, Bohr's own favourite example of the two-slit experiment, in which there appear particles whose distribution has a wave character.) I support de Broglie's pilot waves – hence, the much simpler hypothesis that there are both particles *and* waves, and that material particles are steered by immaterial waves whose amplitudes define probabilistic *tendencies* – or *propensities*, as I have called them.[2] This means that, as in Kepler, it is resonance – and thus harmony and dissonance – which govern the world. Some years ago, especially when I was planning *The Self and Its Brain* together with Sir John Eccles,[3] I followed up the metaphysical hypothesis that it may be possible to solve the body–mind problem by assuming that mind is the highly complex and constantly changing system of propensities described by the wave function of the brain. This metaphysical hypothesis may be described as an attempt to extend the famous theory of Simmias in Plato's *Phaedo*, that is, the Pythagorean theory that regards the mind as the harmony of the body.

I suspect that some of those listening to me will be astonished, even angered, by my enthusiastic approval of Kepler's metaphysical hypotheses. For I have long been branded as a typical Vienna Circle positivist and enemy of metaphysics. Just a few years ago, an American psychologist and brain scientist even wrote in praise: 'Popper is one of the most influential heirs of Mach's emphasis on sensation and of the resulting positivism of the Vienna Circle' (Karl H. Pribram, in *Mind and Brain*, ed. by Sir John Eccles, 1984). It is not at all unlikely, then, that some will diagnose as the folly of old age my evidently opportunist shift from positivism to friendliness towards metaphysics.

Now, the folly-of-old-age diagnosis may well be right, but not the idea that I have changed my views. For in the first paper I ever published in the philosophy of science, in 1933, and again and again since then, I have stressed against positivism (and against its journal *Erkenntnis*) that natural science originated historically as a kind of precipitate of metaphysical ideas. I was mainly thinking then, as I still do today, of the atomic theory of Leucippus and Democritus. That paper that appeared in 1933, the year in which I announced my *Logik der Forschung*, was only two pages or so long. I could therefore discuss in it only the ideas that seemed to me most important. And these ideas were: first, a refutation of Schlick and Wittgenstein; and second, the thesis that scientific theories often originate historically from metaphysics, from which they differ in being its falsifiable precipitates.

My whole methodology consists in the realization that the natural sciences try to find a reality *hidden behind appearances*; that whenever we know nothing we must guess, just as Kepler did; and that if we want to subject our testable hypotheses to the strict test of experience, as Kepler did, these hypotheses are no longer metaphysical hypotheses but become scientific hypotheses that enable us to learn from our mistakes. This is what Kepler did when he eliminated his mistakes and learnt from them. He discovered the most important mistake – the hypothesis of the circular orbit of all heavenly bodies, which was an old dogma – by comparing it with Tycho Brahe's observations.

Kepler himself said at least ten times that what he was doing was *refuting things*. Again and again, he said of a hypothesis he had invented and soon discarded that it was *refuted* by Tycho's observations and that he would therefore have to invent and try out a new hypothesis.

This is how he arrived at refutation, or falsification, of the circular orbit hypothesis; and so, after many further refutations that he explicitly called refutations, he finally reached the elliptical hypothesis. A full statement of it came not in the *Astronomia Nova*, nor even ten years later in the *Harmonices Mundi*, but only in the 'Handbook of Copernican Astronomy', the *Epitome* published in 1620.

It has often been pointed out that Kepler did not set too much store by the first two of Kepler's laws. Why was this? He wanted to uncover the heavenly mechanics, the truth, the reality behind appearances; he sought not merely a better description but a causal explanation, a physics of the heavens. He sought precisely what Newton actually achieved some sixty years later. And he knew that he had not yet achieved it.

What held him back? He had intuitively reached integral calculus, but not differential calculus. He understood that bodies attract and move each other, and that the great force proceeding from the sun is the cause that explains planetary motion. But he did not yet grasp the subtle distinction between a cause of the motion of bodies and a cause of change in their actual state of motion. That is the difference between the Keplerian and Newtonian approaches to the problem of uncovering the *causes* behind appearances, behind Kepler's laws. This gave Kepler the hope that he would find the cause in harmony.

Erhard Oeser has drawn my attention to the fact that Arnold Sommerfeld already noticed a connection between quantum mechanics and Kepler's theory of harmony. This is news to me. But this information, for which I am grateful to Oeser, came too late to be worked into my remarks.

Let me briefly summarize my thesis. Kepler was not, as is so often thought, a man who combined a half-wild, primitive medieval metaphysics with 'modern scientific induction'. Newton erred in believing that Kepler had derived his three laws inductively from Tycho's observations. Kepler, like every scientist, was guided by intuition, by trial (hypothesis) and error (empirical refutation). And like every scientist who seeks and finds something new, he was a metaphysician able to learn from his mistakes. All of this was as clear as daylight to him, whereas many scientists today have still not grasped it.

Without intuition we get nowhere – even though most of our intuitions eventually turn out wrong. We need intuitions, ideas, if possible, competing ideas; and we need ideas about how those ideas can be criticized, improved, and critically tested. And until they are refuted (indeed, for longer), we must also put up with questionable ideas. For even the best ideas are questionable.

Notes

1 On Kepler's theory of music, see the important book by H.F. Cohen, *Quantifying Music*, D. Reidel, Dordrecht, Lancaster, 1984.

2 See my books *The Logic of Scientific Discovery* (Routledge, London, 1959, first published in German in 1934); *Quantum Theory and the Schism in Physics* (Hutchinson, London, 1982); and now also *A World of Propensities* (Thoemmes, Bristol, 1990).

3 Karl Popper and John Eccles, *The Self and Its Brain* (first published by Springer Verlag, Berlin 1977), Routledge, London, 1983.

Part II

THOUGHTS ON
HISTORY AND POLITICS

7

ON FREEDOM*

I

We know little about the human settlement of the Austrian, Swiss, and French Alps, which goes back to prehistoric times. But we really ought to consider how it was that people who farmed and raised livestock moved into the wild, impassable valleys of the High Alps, where to begin with they could at best eke out a hard, meagre, and risk-filled existence. The most likely explanation is that these people preferred an uncertain life in the wilds to subjugation by more powerful neighbours. Despite the uncertainty and the danger, they chose freedom. I often like to play with the idea that the Swiss and Tyrolean tradition of freedom, in particular, goes back to those days of the prehistoric settlement of Switzerland.

It is in any case an interesting and striking fact that Britain and Switzerland, the two oldest democracies of contemporary Europe, are today so similar in their love of freedom and their readiness to defend it. For in many other respects, especially in their political origins, these two democracies are fundamentally different. British democracy owes its emergence to a sense of pride and independence among the upper nobility and, in its later development, to the Protestant mentality, personal conscience, and religious toleration – consequences of the great religious and political conflicts associated with the Puritan Revolution. Swiss democracy resulted not from the pride, independence, and individualism of an upper nobility, but from the pride, independence, and individualism of mountain farmers.

---

* Seminar paper given at Alpach on 25 August 1958. First published in *Die Philosophie und die Wissenschaften. Simon Moser zum 65. Geburtstag,* Anton Hain, Meisenheim am Glan, 1967.

These completely different beginnings and traditions have led to quite different traditional institutions and quite different traditional systems of values. What a Swiss, or Tyrolean, expects or hopes for from life is, I think, generally very different from what a Briton expects or hopes for from life. The difference in value systems is probably based in part upon the difference in educational systems; but it is very interesting that the difference in educational systems is itself deeply rooted in those historical and social oppositions to which I have referred. In England, well into the present century, education was a privilege of the nobility and landowners – the squirearchy; not, that is, of urban dwellers and burghers but of big landowning families living on the land. These families were the bearers of culture. From them too came the private scholars and the scientists (often influential and original amateurs) and the members of the higher professions – politicians, clergymen, judges, military officers. By contrast, the main bearers of culture on the Continent were town-dwellers; they mostly came from the urban bourgeoisie. Education and culture were not things one inherited; they were things one acquired for oneself. Education and culture were not a symbol of inherited social position but a means and a symbol of social advancement, of self-emancipation through knowledge. This also explains why the victorious struggle against poverty in Britain was a kind of continuation of the religious struggles on a different level – a struggle in which the appeal of aristocrats and townspeople to religious conscience played a decisive role – whereas the struggle against poverty in Switzerland and Austria was inspired by the idea of self-emancipation through knowledge, by Pestalozzi's great vision of education.

Despite all these deep differences, both Britain and Switzerland know that there are values that must be defended at any price, and chief among these values are personal independence, personal freedom. And both have learnt that freedom has to be fought for, and that one must stand by it even if the probability of success appears minute. In 1940, when Britain was battling alone for freedom, Churchill did not promise victory to the British. 'I can promise you nothing better than blood and tears', he said. Those words gave Britain the courage to keep on fighting.

In Switzerland, too, it was only a traditional determination to struggle – even against a clearly superior enemy, such as the Habsburgs and later the Third Reich – that enabled the Swiss to retain their freedom during the Second World War.

II

I fear that the magnificent surroundings of our dear Alpbach, this wonderful interplay of nature and human hand, of love of one's native land and hard work, have made my opening words a little sentimental and romantic. I therefore feel immediately obliged to offset these sentimental, romantic words with a second introduction directed against romanticism – especially romanticism in philosophy. I would like to begin this second introduction with a confession.

It is especially important to me that what I am about to say is not taken on trust. Indeed, I should prefer it to be treated with the utmost scepticism. Unlike so many of my philosophical colleagues, I am not a leader travelling on new paths, heralding new directions in philosophy. I am a thoroughly old-fashioned philosopher who believes in a completely outmoded philosophy: that is, the philosophy of an age long past, the age of rationalism and the Enlightenment. As one of the last stragglers of rationalism and the Enlightenment, I believe in human self-emancipation through knowledge – just as Kant, the greatest philosopher of the Enlightenment, once did, or as Pestalozzi used knowledge to fight against poverty. I should therefore like to say quite clearly that I represent views that were already seen as outdated and totally mistaken some 150 years ago. For it was a little before 1800 that Romanticism exposed the Enlightenment [*die Aufklärung*] as mere 'scouting around' [*Aufklärerei*], or as *Aufkläricht* – an allusion to *Kehricht* or 'garbage'. But unfortunately I am so much behind the times that I still cling to this obsolete, outmoded philosophy. Being so backward, I cannot see the philosophy of romanticism – particularly that of the three principal leaders of German Idealism, Fichte, Schelling, and Hegel – as anything other than an intellectual and moral catastrophe, the greatest intellectual and moral catastrophe with which German and European intellectuals have so far been afflicted. In my opinion, this intellectual and moral catastrophe had a devastating and stultifying effect that is still spreading like an atomic cloud. It brought about what Konrad Heiden, in his book on Hitler, called some years ago 'the age of intellectual and moral dishonesty'.

It is a Zeitgeist, and a Zeitgeist-inspired movement, that will not be so easy for anyone to stop – least of all for a late Enlightenment straggler such as myself, who is well aware of the power of fashion or the Zeitgeist but is not willing to make any concessions to it. In contrast to the great Romantic and contemporary authorities, I do not believe it is a philosopher's task to express the spirit of his age. I believe (as Nietzsche also did) that a philosopher should be continually checking whether he has not after all started to make concessions to the Zeitgeist which put his intellectual independence at risk. I fully agree with Hugo von Hofmannsthal when he says in his *Buch der Freunde*: 'Philosophy must be a *judge* of her times; things are in a bad way when she becomes an *expression* of the spirit of her times.'

III

My accusations against myself, and my confession that I am a rationalist and a man of the Enlightenment, would have little point if I did not briefly explain what I understand by rationalism and Enlightenment.

When I speak of rationalism, I am not thinking of a philosophical theory (such as Descartes's) and not at all of the highly unreasonable belief that man is a purely rational creature. When I speak of reason or rationalism, all I mean is the conviction that we can *learn* through criticism of our mistakes and errors, especially through criticism by others, and eventually also through self-criticism. A rationalist is simply someone for whom it is more important to learn than to be proved right; someone who is willing to learn from others – not by simply taking over another's opinions, but by gladly allowing others to criticize his ideas and by gladly criticizing the ideas of others. The emphasis here is on the idea of criticism or, to be more precise, *critical discussion*. The genuine rationalist does not think that he or anyone else is in possession of the truth; nor does he think that mere criticism as such helps us to achieve new ideas. But he does think that, in the sphere of ideas, only critical discussion can help us sort the wheat from the chaff. He is well aware that acceptance or rejection of an idea is never a purely rational matter; but he thinks that only critical discussion can give us the necessary maturity to see an idea from more and more sides and to make a correct judgement of it.

This assessment of critical discussion also has its human side. For the rationalist knows perfectly well that critical discussion is not the only relationship between people: that, on the contrary, rational critical discussion is a rare phenomenon in our lives. Yet he thinks that the 'give and take' attitude fundamental to critical discussion is of the greatest purely human significance. For the rationalist knows that he owes his reason to other people. He knows that the rational critical attitude can only be the result of others' criticism, and that only through others' criticism can one arrive at self-criticism.

The rationalist approach might be described as follows. Perhaps I am wrong and you are right; anyway we can both hope that after our discussion we will both see things more clearly than before, just so long as we remember that our drawing closer to the truth is more important than the question of who is right. Only with this goal in mind do we defend ourselves as well as we can in discussion.

This, in short, is what I mean when I speak of rationalism. But when I speak of Enlightenment, I mean something else as well. I think above all of the idea of self-emancipation through knowledge, the idea that Kant and Pestalozzi inspired. And I think of the duty of every intellectual to help others to free their minds and to understand the critical approach – a duty which most intellectuals have forgotten since the time of Fichte, Schelling, and Hegel. For unfortunately, it is all too common among intellectuals to want to impress others and, as Schopenhauer put it, not to teach but to captivate. They appear as leaders or prophets – partly because it is expected of them to appear as prophets, as proclaimers of the dark secrets of life and the world, of man, history, and existence. Here, as so often, ceaseless demand produces a supply. Leaders and prophets are looked for, so it is hardly surprising that leaders and prophets are found. But 'grown men do not need leaders', as H.G. Wells once said. And grown men ought to *know* that they do not need leaders. As for prophets, I believe in the duty of every intellectual to keep them at arm's length.

IV

What externally distinguishes the Enlightenment approach and the approach of self-declared prophets? It is language. The Enlightenment thinker speaks as simply as possible. He wants to be understood. In this respect Bertrand Russell is our unsurpassed master among philosophers. Even when you cannot agree with him, you have to admire him. He always speaks so clearly, simply, and directly.

Why does simplicity of language matter so much to Enlightenment thinkers? Because the true Enlightenment thinker, the true rationalist, never wants to talk anyone into anything. No, he does not even want to convince: all the time he is aware that he may be wrong. Above all, he values the intellectual independence of others too highly to want to convince them in important matters. He would much rather invite contradiction, preferably in the form of rational and disciplined criticism. He seeks not to convince but to arouse – to challenge others to form free opinions. Free opinion formation is precious to him: not only because this brings us all closer to the truth, but also because he respects free opinion formation as such. He respects it even when he considers the opinion so formed to be fundamentally wrong.

One of the reasons why the Enlightenment thinker does not want to talk people into anything, or even to convince them, is the following. He knows that, outside the narrow field of logic and perhaps mathematics, nothing can ever be proved. One can certainly put forward arguments, and one can critically examine points of view. But outside elementary mathematics, our arguments are never conclusive and free of gaps. We must always weigh up the reasons, always decide which reasons carry more weight: those in favour of a certain point of view, or those against it. In the end, then, opinion formation contains an element of free decision. And it is the free decision that makes an opinion humanly precious.

It was from John Locke that the Enlightenment took and developed this high esteem for free personal opinion. It was doubtless the direct result of the English and Continental religious struggles, which eventually brought forth the idea of religious toleration. And this idea of religious toleration is by no means a merely negative idea, as so many (e.g., Arnold Toynbee) have claimed. It is not only an expression of war weariness and of a realization that terror offers no prospect of imposing a conformity of religious belief. Rather, religious toleration springs from the exact opposite: from a positive understanding that forced religious unanimity is completely worthless; that *only* freely assumed religious belief can be of any value. And this realization leads further. It leads to respect for any honest belief, and hence to respect for the individual and his opinion. In the words of Immanuel Kant, the last great philosopher of the Enlightenment, it leads to recognition of the value of the human person.

In talking of the value of the human person, Kant meant that every human being and his convictions should be respected. Kant combined this precept with the Hillelian principle, which in English is rightly called the golden rule but in German sounds rather banal: 'Do not do unto others what you would not have them do unto you!' Kant closely associated this principle with the idea of freedom – the freedom of thought demanded by Schiller's Marquis de Posa of Philipp II; the freedom of thought that Spinoza sought to justify by claiming it as an inalienable freedom that tyrants, however much they try, can never actually wrest from us.

I think we can no longer agree with Spinoza about this. Perhaps it is true that freedom of thought can never be completely suppressed, but it can be suppressed to quite a considerable degree. For without a free exchange of ideas there can be no true freedom of thought. To find out whether our ideas are sound, we need other people to try them out on. Critical discussion is the basis of free thought for each individual. This means, however, that freedom of thought is impossible without political freedom. And it also means that political freedom is a precondition of the free use of reason by each individual.

I have tried to explain briefly what I understand by rationalism and Enlightenment. At the same time, I have tried briefly to indicate why rationalism as I understand it, as well as Enlightenment, requires freedom of thought, religious freedom, respect for other people's honest opinions, and finally political freedom. But I am very far from claiming that only rationalism loves freedom or can give reasons for demanding it. On the contrary, I am convinced there are quite different attitudes, especially religious attitudes, that demand freedom of conscience and that, taking this demand further, also arrive at respect for the opinions of others and a justification of the demand for political freedom. And if I earlier, perhaps a little ironically, warned of my outdated rationalism, I would now like to repeat this warning in all seriousness. Because I am a rationalist, I do not want to convert anybody. Nor do I want to abuse the name of freedom to turn anyone else into a rationalist. But I should like to challenge others to contradict me; I should like, if possible, to prompt others to see things in a new light, so that each may take his *own* decision in the freest possible formation of opinion. Every rationalist must say with Kant: one cannot teach philosophy – at most only philosophizing, which means a critical attitude.

V

Of course, we do not know for certain where this philosophizing, this critical attitude, originated. But everything suggests it is very rare, and so it can lay claim to scarcity value (apart from other values). As far as we know, it originated in Greece and was invented by Thales of Miletus, the founder of the Ionian school of natural philosophy.

There are schools even among quite primitive peoples. The task of a school is always to preserve and pass on the teachings of its founder. If a member of the school tries to change the doctrine, he is expelled as a heretic and the school splits. Thus the number of schools generally increases through splits. But sometimes, of course, the school's traditional doctrine must adapt to new external conditions – for example, to newly acquired knowledge that has become common property. In such cases, the change in the school's official doctrine is nearly always introduced surreptitiously through a reinterpretation of the old doctrine, so that it can later be said that nothing has actually changed in the doctrine. The newly altered doctrine (which is not said to have been altered) is attributed to the master who originally founded the school. 'The master himself said' is what we constantly hear in the Pythagorean school.

It is therefore usually impossible, or uncommonly difficult, to reconstruct the history of the ideas of such a school. For it is an essential part of the method that all ideas are attributed to the founder. To my knowledge, the only school tradition that deviates from this rigid schema is the tradition of the Ionian school of Thales, which over time became the tradition of Greek philosophy and eventually, after the revival of this philosophy in the Renaissance, the tradition of European science.

Let us try for a moment to imagine what it means to break with the dogmatic tradition of *one* pure school doctrine, and to replace it with a tradition of critical debate, a tradition of pluralism in which many competing doctrines all attempt to draw closer to a single truth.

That it was Thales who took this truly epochal step, may be seen from the fact that in the Ionian school, and only in the Ionian school, members quite openly attempted to improve the master's doctrine. We can understand this only if we imagine Thales saying to his followers: 'This is my teaching. This is how I conceive of things. Try to improve it.'

In this way Thales created a new tradition – a two-layer tradition, as it were. First, his own doctrine was passed on by the school tradition, as were the differing doctrines of each new generation of followers. Second, a tradition was preserved of criticizing one's own teacher and trying to do better. In this school, then, the changing or overcoming of a doctrine counted as a success; and such a change was recorded with the name of the person who introduced it. This made a real history of ideas possible for the first time.

The two-layer tradition I have described is the tradition of our modern science. It is one of the most important elements of our Western world. To my knowledge, it was invented only once. It was lost after two or three hundred years, but rediscovered by the Renaissance – essentially by Galileo Galilei – after another one and a half thousand years. It is thus quite possible for it to be destroyed and forgotten. And it can fully develop only where there is political freedom.

Although rationalism, as I have outlined it here, is still a very rare thing even in Europe and can hardly be regarded as one of Europe's characteristic religions, and although the ideas of rationalism are nowadays treated with sovereign contempt by most intellectuals, the rationalism of Thales is nevertheless an idea and a tradition without which our European civilization would not exist at all. For nothing is as characteristic of our European civilization as its zeal for science. It is the only civilization to have produced natural science, and the only one where this plays a quite decisive role. But natural science is the direct product of rationalism; it is the product of the rationalism of ancient Greek philosophy.

VI

All I have done so far is present myself as a rationalist and follower of the Enlightenment, and try to explain what I mean when I speak of rationalism and Enlightenment. I have also briefly indicated that rationalism and Enlightenment postulate political freedom. But it would be ridiculous to identify the love of freedom with rationalism or Enlightenment, or even to assert a very close relationship between them.

The desire for freedom is certainly something primeval, which we already find in widely varying degrees among animals – even domestic animals – and in young children. But freedom becomes a problem in the domain of politics. For human coexistence naturally means that unlimited freedom for each individual is an impossibility. If I am free to do anything I want, I am also free to rob others of their freedom.

Kant's solution was to demand that the state should limit individual freedom only to the extent made necessary by human coexistence, and that this necessary limitation should apply to all citizens as equally as possible. This genuinely Kantian principle shows that the problem of political freedom is at least conceptually solvable. But it does not provide us with a criterion of political freedom. For often in individual cases, we cannot establish whether a certain limitation of freedom is really necessary, nor whether it is a burden imposed equally on all citizens. We therefore need another criterion that can be more easily applied. My own proposal for one is the following. *A state is politically free if its political institutions enable its citizens in practice to change a government without bloodshed when a majority wishes such a change.* Or, more succinctly: we are free if we can get rid of our rulers without bloodshed.

Here we have a criterion that allows us to distinguish political freedom from lack of political freedom or, if you like, a democracy from a tyranny.

Of course, nothing hangs on the *words* 'democracy' and 'tyranny'. If, for example, someone called certain unfree states 'democracies' and the constitution of the United Kingdom or Switzerland a 'tyranny', I would not get involved in a dispute over whether these terms are right or wrong. I would simply say: 'If I had to use your terminology, I would have to describe myself as an enemy of democracy and a friend of tyranny.' This allows one to avoid getting lost in terminological disputes; the important thing is not words but real values.

The criterion of political freedom I have just offered is a simple, but of course somewhat crude, instrument. In particular, it tells us nothing about the very important question of the protection of minorities – for example, of religious, linguistic, or ethnic minorities.

VII

With everything I have said so far, I have been trying to create something like a framework in which to address a few more topical questions concerning the present situation of freedom and the free Western world. I should formulate the central such question as follows:

What has freedom brought us? Good or evil? Which is there more of? What do the scales of good and evil reveal?

I find this a highly stimulating question, and I shall try to answer it as clearly and concisely as possible in a set of theses.

My *first thesis* is that our world, the world of Western democracies, may not be the best of all conceivable or logically possible political worlds, but it is the best of all political worlds of whose existence we have any historical knowledge. In this respect, then, I am a wild optimist.

To explain and justify this optimistic first thesis of mine, let me first say that I am not thinking mainly of the booming economic miracle when I praise our times, although it is certainly no small detail that in our society fewer people go hungry than ever before. What I have in mind is something quite different. Perhaps I can best explain this by drawing a contrast. In 1942 the former Bishop of Bradford condemned our Western world as Satan's world and called upon all faithful ministers of the Christian religions to take part in erasing this work of the devil and in helping Stalin's communism to victory. Since then, Stalin's satanic character has been recognized by the communists themselves, and for a short but most refreshing period his satanic character was a major component of the general line of the Party, if not quite of the Party programme. Yet there are still believers – and in Britain, even genuinely devout Christians – who still think as the former Bishop of Bradford used to do.

To express clearly my first, optimistic thesis, I should like to say that from precisely the same standpoint as the one from which the Bishop condemned our Western world as the devil's work, I describe it as the best of all the worlds of which we have any historical knowledge.

For the Bishop it was mainly a question of purely human values – what Kant called human dignity and human readiness to help. These, he thought, were at risk in the West and assured in Russia. But it seems to me that, in his idealism, he did not see the facts properly. Never before has there been a society in which there is so little repression, in which so few people are humiliated and insulted, as in our own society. Never before have so many been prepared to make sacrifices to relieve the hunger and misery of others.

I think therefore that we in the West have no reason to be ashamed in relation to the East. But I do not say that we in the West should not criticize our institutions – on the contrary. Although our world is the best there has so far been, many things in it are in a really bad way. And what we have achieved can be lost at any time: this is and will always remain a great danger. I come now to my *second* thesis.

Although I consider our political world to be the best of which we have any historical knowledge, we should beware of attributing this fact to democracy or freedom. Freedom is not a supplier who delivers life's goods to our door. Democracy does not ensure that anything is accomplished – certainly not an economic miracle. It is wrong and extremely dangerous to extol freedom by telling people that they will certainly be all right once they are free. How someone fares in life is largely a matter of luck or grace, and to a comparatively small degree perhaps also of competence, diligence, and other virtues. The most one can say of democracy or freedom is that they give our personal abilities a little more influence on our well-being. This brings me to my *third* thesis.

We should choose political freedom not because we hope for an easier life but because freedom is itself an ultimate value that cannot be reduced to material values. We must choose it in the manner of Democritus, who once said: 'I prefer a meagre existence in a democracy to riches under a tyranny'; and 'The poverty of a democracy is better than every wealth under an aristocracy or autocracy, for freedom is better than slavery'.

In my *fourth* thesis I should like to go a step further. Freedom, democracy, and our own belief in them can become disastrous for us.

It is wrong to think that belief in freedom always leads to victory; we must always be prepared for it to lead to defeat. If we choose freedom, then we must be prepared to perish along with it. Poland fought for freedom as no other country did. The Czech nation was prepared to fight for its freedom in 1938: it was not lack of courage that sealed its fate. The Hungarian Revolution of 1956 – the work of young people with nothing to lose but their chains – triumphed and then ended in failure.

The struggle for freedom may also fail in other ways. It may degenerate into terrorism, as in the French and Russian Revolutions. It may lead to extreme bondage. Democracy and freedom do not guarantee the millennium. No, we do not choose political freedom because it promises us this or that. We choose it because it makes possible the only dignified form of human coexistence, the only form in which we can be fully responsible for ourselves. Whether we realize its possibilities depends on all kinds of things – and above all on ourselves.

8

ON THE THEORY OF
DEMOCRACY*

My greatest interest is in nature – and natural science or cosmology. Once I gave up Marxism in July 1919, I was interested in politics and political theory only as a citizen – and a democrat. But the totalitarian movements of Left and Right that arose in the 1920s and early 1930s, and finally Hitler's seizure of power in Germany, forced me to give considerable thought to the problem of democracy.

Although my book *The Open Society and Its Enemies* did not once mention Hitler and the Nazis, it was intended as my contribution to the war against them. It is a theoretical defence of democracy against the old and new attacks of its enemies; it was first published in 1945 and has since been through many editions. But what I regard as its most important point seems not often to be properly understood.

As everyone knows, 'democracy' etymologically means 'rule by the people' or 'popular sovereignty', in contradistinction to 'aristocracy' (rule by the best or most distinguished) and 'monarchy' (rule by one individual). But the meaning of the word is not of any further help to us. For the people do not rule anywhere; it is always governments that rule (and unfortunately also bureaucrats or officials, who can be held accountable only with difficulty, if at all). Besides, Great Britain, Denmark, Norway, and Sweden are monarchies but also very good examples of democracies (except for Sweden perhaps, where an unaccountable fiscal bureaucracy exercises dictatorial powers) – quite unlike the German Democratic Republic, which unfortunately is nothing of the kind.

What is really at issue here?

---

* First published in *Der Spiegel* No. 32, 3 August 1987, pp. 54f.

There are in fact only two forms of state: those in which it is possible to get rid of a government without bloodshed, and those in which this is not possible. This is what matters – not what the form of state is called. Usually the first form is called 'democracy' and the second 'dictatorship' or 'tyranny'. But it is not worth arguing over words (such as the German 'Democratic' Republic). All that counts is whether the government can be removed without bloodshed.

There are a number of such ways in which the government might be removed. The best method is a ballot: fresh elections or a vote in an already elected parliament can bring a government down. That certainly matters. It is therefore wrong to put the stress (as so many from Plato to Marx and even later have done) on the question: 'Who should rule? The people (the proletariat) or the very best? The (good) workers or the (evil) capitalists? The majority or the minority? The party of the Left, the party of the Right or the party of the Centre?' All these questions are wrongly posed. For it does not matter who rules if it is possible to get rid of the government without bloodshed. Any government that can be thrown out has a strong incentive to act in a way that makes people content with it. And this incentive is lost if the government knows it cannot be so easily ousted.

To show how important this simple theory of democracy is in practice, I should like to apply it to the problem of proportional representation. If I here criticize an electoral system anchored in the Federal Republic's well-tried constitution, this should be seen simply as an attempt on my part to discuss something that is rarely discussed. Constitutions should not be changed lightly, but it is good to discuss them critically, if only so that we remain aware of their importance.

The democracies of continental Western Europe differ crucially from the electoral systems of the United Kingdom and the United States, which are based upon the principle of local representation. In Britain each constituency sends as its representative to Parliament the person who has gained the highest number of votes. Which party he belongs to, and indeed whether he belongs to one at all, is not officially taken into consideration. His duty is to represent his local constituents to the best of his knowledge and belief, whether or not they belong to any party. There are parties, of course, and they play a major role in the formation of governments. But if a representative thinks it is in his constituency's (or perhaps the nation's) interest for him to vote against his party, or even to break from it, he has an obligation to do so. Winston Churchill, the greatest statesman of our century, never simply toed the line and indeed twice changed his party. The situation is quite different on the Continent.

Proportionality means that each party gets that number of representatives in parliament – in the Bundestag, for example – that most closely represents the votes cast for it in the country.

In this way parties are constitutionally anchored in the basic laws, and individual deputies are officially selected to represent their party. A deputy, then, cannot in certain circumstances have a duty to vote against his party. Indeed, he is morally bound to his party because he has been chosen to represent it and it alone. (Should he no longer be able to square this with his conscience, he has a moral duty to resign – even if the constitution does not require him to.)

I know, of course, that parties are needed: no one has yet come up with a democratic system that can manage without them. But political parties are not altogether satisfactory. On the other hand, things do not work without them. Our democracies are not people's governments but party governments – that is, party leaders' governments. For the larger the party, the less united and the less democratic it is, and the less influence those who voted for it have upon the party's leadership and programme. It is wrong to think that a parliament elected by proportional representation is a better reflection of the people and its wishes. It does not represent the people and its views but simply the influence that the various parties (and party propaganda) had upon the electorate on polling day. And it makes it more difficult for polling day to be what it could and should be: a day when the people judge the activity of the government.

There is no valid theory of popular sovereignty, then, no valid theory that requires proportional representation. We must therefore ask ourselves how proportional representation works out in practice: first, in the formation of governments, and second, in the crucially important matter of their removal.

1. The more parties there are, the more difficult it is to form a government. We know this from experience, but it also stands to reason. When there are only two parties, a government can easily be formed. But proportional representation makes it possible even for small parties to gain great (often decisive) influence over the formation of a government, and thus even over the government's decisions.

Everyone will agree that this is so, and everyone knows that proportional representation increases the number of parties. But so long as one takes the 'essence' of democracy to be popular sovereignty, one has to swallow these problems as a democrat because proportionality appears to be 'essential'.

2. Proportional representation, and therefore the multiplicity of parties, may have even worse consequences in the important matter of a

government's removal by the people's verdict in new parliamentary elections. First, people know that there are many parties and therefore hardly expect one of them to gain an absolute majority. So when things turn out as expected, the people's verdict has not actually been expressed against any of the parties. None of them has been thrown out, none has had judgement passed upon it.

Second, election day is not expected to be a day when the people judge the government. Sometimes it may have been a minority government, forced to make concessions and unable to do what it considered right; or else it may have been a coalition government for which none of the ruling parties was fully responsible.

By and by, people get used to holding none of the political parties, and none of their leaders, responsible for the decisions taken by the government. The fact that a party loses perhaps five or ten per cent of its vote is not seen by anyone as a guilty verdict – or at least not by the voters, not by the governed. All that it indicates is a momentary wavering in popularity.

Third, if a majority of voters want to throw out a majority government, it may not be possible for them to do it. For even if a party that has so far had an absolute majority (and could therefore be held responsible) loses its majority, it will still most probably be the largest single party under the proportional system, and therefore be able to form a coalition government with one of the smaller parties. In that case, the dismissed leader of the main party will continue to govern against the decision of the majority, by relying upon a small party that may be miles from representing 'the will of the people'. Moreover, such a small party may also bring down a government without new elections, without a fresh mandate from the electorate, and then form a different coalition government with the erstwhile opposition parties – in grotesque contradiction to the basic idea of proportional representation, which is that a party's influence should correspond to the number of its voters.

Such outcomes are frequent, and have come to be taken for granted where a large number of parties means that coalition governments are the rule.

It is quite true that similar things can happen in countries that do not have proportional representation – in the United Kingdom or the United States, for example. But there a tendency has developed for two major parties to compete with each other.

A form of elections that makes the two-party system possible seems to me the best form of democracy. For it always leads to self-criticism by the parties. If one of two major parties suffers disastrous defeat at the polls, this usually leads to radical changes within the party. It is a result of competition, and of clear condemnation by the electorate that cannot be disregarded. Under such a system, then, parties are from time to time forced to learn from their mistakes or to go under. My remarks against proportional representation do not mean that I advise all democracies to give it up. I only want to give a new impetus to the debate. To think that the moral superiority of proportional representation can be logically derived from the idea of democracy, and that the Continental system is for this reason better, fairer, or more democratic than the Anglo-Saxon one, is a naive view that does not stand up to close scrutiny.

To sum up: the argument that proportional representation is more democratic than the British or American system is not tenable, because it has to refer to an outdated theory of democracy as government by the people (which rests in turn upon the so-called sovereignty theory of the state). This theory is morally defective and even unsustainable. It has been superseded by the theory of majority power of dismissal.

This moral argument is even more important than the practical argument that no more than two fully accountable competing parties are required to enable voters to sit in judgement on a government. Proportional representation creates the danger that the majority verdict at the polls, and hence the effect of defeat upon parties that is beneficial to democracy, will be regarded as a trivial detail. For there to be a clear majority verdict, it is important that the opposition party should be as good and strong as possible. Otherwise the voters are often forced to let a bad government go on governing, because they have reason to think that 'nothing else will be any better'.

Does my defence of the two-party system not conflict with the idea of an open society? Is not pluralist toleration of many views and theories characteristic of the open society and its quest for truth? Should this pluralism not be expressed in a multiplicity of parties? In reply, I should say that it is the function of a political party either to form a government or, in opposition, to keep a critical watch on the work of the government. One of the things to be critically watched is the government's toleration of various opinions, ideologies, and religions (in so far as these are themselves tolerant, for ideologies that preach intolerance lose their claim to be tolerated). Many ideologies will attempt, with or without success, to dominate a party or to found a new one. So there will be an interplay of opinions, ideologies, and religions, on the one side, and the main competing parties on the other.

But the idea that the variety of ideologies or world-views should be reflected in a multiplicity of parties appears to me politically misconceived – and not only politically but also as a view of the world. For too close an association with party politics is hardly compatible with the purity of a world-view.

9

ALL LIFE IS PROBLEM SOLVING*

I

I am almost as old as the motor car. I was not yet born when it was invented in 1886, but I was already a year old when Kaiser Wilhelm II (of whom I have a clear memory) acquired his first car.

My first car journey to Schloss Altenberg, near Greifenstein on the Danube, was in a Mercedes belonging to the owner of the castle, a friend of my father's. Previously we had always been collected by a coach and four, but this time I was told we were going in a Mercedes, the best German motor car and the first of this model to be imported into Austria. It must have been 1907 or 1908.

I bought my first (second-hand) car in 1936 in London. I immediately drove it to Cambridge, and when I got out – on the right side, of course – I noticed that the rear wheel and its axle were protruding quite a bit from the car. As I recall, some thirty centimetres of axle could be seen, but my astonishment may well have coloured my memory. It was a 'Standard' sports car, a make that has long since disappeared – and rightly so.

These experiences are some of the unrepeatable advantages of old age. Another is that, unlike my younger contemporaries, I think that our world and the human beings in it are both wonderful. Of course, I know there are also a lot of bad things in our world, and yet it is still the best there has ever been in history. When I say this, those listening usually treat me as if I were senile. That may well be true, but in the coming discussion I am prepared to defend myself against anyone and argue that the general moaning about the evil world in which we live – which may be called the dominant religion of our times – is in

* Lecture given in Bad Homburg in 1991.

conflict with all the facts. My main thesis is that not only are we doing better economically, we are also morally better. One thing I am willing to admit: that we are more stupid than ever before, and uncritical of whatever is thought of as modern. But that is never pleasant to hear, and will certainly not be believed.

Perhaps the reason for this is the terrible mistakes we make as teachers, and since education may be classed as technology, these are technological mistakes. The worst of it is that we learn nothing from these mistakes – which brings me to my real topic today.

Error correction is the most important method in technology and learning in general. In biological evolution, it appears to be the only means of progress. One rightly speaks of the trial-and-error method, but this understates the importance of mistakes or errors – of the erroneous trial.

Biological evolution is full of mistakes, and their correction takes place slowly. So we may excuse our many mistakes by recalling that they only imitate sweet verdant Nature – and that we usually correct them rather faster than verdant Nature does. For some of us consciously try to learn from our mistakes. All scientists, technologists, and technicians do this, for example, or at least they ought to do it. For that is precisely what their profession requires.

Life, beginning with unicellular organisms, invents the most astonishing things. New inventions or mutations are usually eliminated, being much more often bad mistakes than successful trials. We may recognize many of our ideas as mistaken before we seriously criticize them, and others may be eliminated through criticism before they reach the production process. In conscious self-criticism and in friendly or hostile criticism made by colleagues or others, we perhaps appear rather superior to Nature. In the trial-and-error method, in the method of selection through critical experiments, Nature has up to now been far superior. Many of its inventions – for example, the conversion of solar energy into an easily storable form of chemical energy – we have so far tried vainly to imitate. But we shall succeed in the foreseeable future.

All life is problem solving. All organisms are inventors and technicians, good or not so good, successful or not so successful, in solving technical problems. This is how it is among animals – spiders, for example. Human technology solves human problems such as sewage disposal, or the storage and supply of food and water, as, for example, bees already have to do.

Hostility to technology, such as we often find among the Greens, is therefore a foolish kind of hostility to life itself – which the Greens have unfortunately not realized. But the critique of technology is not foolish, of course; it is urgently necessary. Everyone is capable of it in their different ways, and most welcome to contribute. And since criticism is an occupational skill of technologists, the critique of technology is a constant preoccupation of theirs.

Nevertheless, it is often outsiders who see a problem first. This may be because an inventor is rightly keen to have his invention applied, and may therefore overlook its possibly undesirable consequences. Thus, certain chemical inventions proved very successful against mosquitoes and other insects, but with the undesirable result that songbirds died of starvation. The American naturalist Rachel Carson reported all this in her excellent book *Silent Spring*, which not surprisingly caused a storm of indignation in America and then in Germany, where a political movement developed against science and technology (and against America) and a new political party, the Greens, was founded.

It is important to draw attention to the little-noticed mistakes that we make. It is understandable that these mistakes are often exaggerated, and perhaps this is necessary to gain a hearing. But to attack science and technology as a whole, when they alone permit the necessary corrections to be made, is not only stupid but sensation-seeking and completely irresponsible.

That some sensation-seekers even go so far as to claim that we are on the brink of the abyss and perhaps need a dictator to save us with Hitler still quite fresh in our memory, can only be described as madness.

It is perfectly true that some problems – air pollution, for example – may require special legislation. There are ideological worshippers of the so-called 'free market' (to which we naturally owe a great deal) who think that such legislation limiting market freedom is a dangerous step down the road to serfdom.

But that again is ideological nonsense. Forty-six years ago in the first edition of *The Open Society and Its Enemies*, I have already shown that a free market can exist only within a legal order created and guaranteed by the state. One element of this order is the ban on armed party organizations, which involves a limitation of the freedom to trade in weapons – and hence of the free market and personal freedom. But clearly, this limitation is imposed by the state preferable to the limitations on freedom that gang leaders would certainly impose in its absence.

We therefore control the arms market for the sake of civil liberty in general, much as we have to restrict the behaviour of wild animals and hunting dogs. The limits of any freedom are always problematic and a matter of experience. Obviously there must be laws against toxic gas emissions in manufacturing industry, and obviously it is a problem to draw a clear distinction between toxic gases and milder forms of air pollution (car exhaust fumes, for instance). The very distinction will, in fact, depend upon such factors as traffic density.

In any event, we must replace the ideological principle of the free market with a different principle: namely, that freedom should be restricted only where there are compelling reasons why it is necessary. And in many cases, there will not be agreement as to what is really necessary.

This kind of situation arises whenever freedom plays a role. By no means does it arise only with problems of the environment or large-scale industry. In reality, all our actions have unintended consequences. Many of these may have been foreseeable with greater effort and cost, but others simply cannot be predicted.

For example, when Otto Hahn and Fritz Strassmann conducted the experiment that was to lead to the splitting of uranium, they could not possibly have foreseen the consequences. They expected nothing of the kind, nor did it occur to them to interpret in that way the observed results, which they found so hard to understand.

The interpretation was a completely new idea that Hahn's discharged assistant Lise Meitner, and her nephew, my friend Otto Robert Frisch, developed in a discussion while on a skiing holiday in Sweden. This completely new idea would scarcely have entered their heads if Frisch the experimenter had not recently started working with the theorist Niels Bohr, who told him of his drop theory of the atomic nucleus and his explanation of the decay of excessively large drops.

Knowledge of this intuitive, and purely metaphorical, aid to understanding played a role in the correct interpretation of Hahn's and Strassmann's experiment – an interpretation completely unavailable to the two devisers of the experiment, who had not in the least expected its outcome.

Here I shall conclude the first part of my remarks – my defence against the attacks on technology – by observing that we all make mistakes, but that nearly everything the Greens lay at the door of technology is actually due to the population explosion. The Greens say too little about this major problem – evidently because it would spoil their attack on technology if they were prepared to investigate it seriously.

II

This second part is not a defence against objections but a eulogy of the place of technology in human culture.

In this connection, I want to distinguish between two categories of invention. First, there are those that help an existing industry to grow: the best example is James Watt's steam engine, whose application created many industries in Britain. We may count such inventions among improved means of production.

To the second category belong the really major cultural inventions. The first of these was human language itself, followed by the various scripts, the written book, the first book market in Athens (around 500 BC), the printed book, the copying machine, the typewriter, the computer, and so on.

It is an amazing but little-known fact that the first copying machine goes back to the same James Watt who invented the steam engine. It is based upon a very simple idea. Perhaps you still remember from your youth the 'blotting paper' that has since been made redundant by quick-drying inks. Watt's idea was essentially to combine an ink that could be moistened again and again, with blotting paper that absorbed it. To avoid the usual mirror effect, he used a specially prepared thin blotting paper that let the ink through and allowed it to be read on the reverse side.

The date of the patent, which covers production of the two sheets of paper and the composition of the ink, is 1780! This invention, the oldest known copying machine, sank into oblivion – if it was ever known at all. It still works today. Although it allows very few copies to be made, it would have been extremely useful to writers, for example. As I was too disturbed by the noise of the old typewriters to get used to typing myself, and as I often find myself losing manuscripts, I can certainly tell you a thing or two about a writer's need for a copying machine. Here we have an example of an unnoticed invention of the greatest potential importance – as culturally significant as the printed book.

Another invention that was for a long time of little more than cultural importance is photography. For many years, it almost exclusively fulfilled the individual need for a portrait. This was a matter not only of a survival wish (one thinks of the Egyptian mummies) but also of the need of family and friends to keep their memories as vivid as possible.

But culturally more important than any of this was the personal need that led to the massive transport revolution: the George

Stephenson Revolution and the still more significant Henry Ford Revolution. (I know Ford was not an inventor, but he did revolutionize America and then the world.)

You could say that the first railways were motorized stagecoaches for people and their luggage; it was not goods wagons but passenger carriages that came first. They addressed a personal need to travel – mainly to see relatives and friends. The same is true of the motor vehicle, and of the revolutionary Model T Ford, which revolutionized the whole of the United States, not only offering or facilitating but actually giving a new way of life to the American people. It was a revolution of the mind that led to a new world-view and new attitudes, more revolutionary than anything one could have expected from a change in the way of life. In effect, it freed everyone from chains of which they had not been aware. The novel of this half-conscious liberation is Sinclair Lewis's *Free Air*.

Perhaps even more important, morally, was the great liberation of domestic slaves (also known as maids), which became possible largely through household mechanization. This tremendous revolution, and the emancipation that all but the very richest women experienced at that time, is today remarkably little remembered, even though it was a liberation from heart-rending slavery. Who today has any idea what it meant when all water had to be fetched and carried, when coal had to be brought in for any heating, when all washing had to be done by hand, when there were still oil lamps with wicks? Then gas was introduced – first only for wretched lighting by butterfly burners, then by the wonderful Auer gas mantle – all that was a purely cultural development.

About 1913 human emancipation – or, to be more precise, female emancipation – slowly began with the gas cooker, and only in 1922 or thereabouts did gas became a serious rival to coal as a kitchen stove fuel. Even central heating systems continued to use coal or coke for a long time.

Such terrible domestic labour must have greatly shortened the life span – not to speak of the suffering at work that is today being replaced by *joie de vivre*. Women owe this to technology, even those who preach hostility towards it.

10

AGAINST
THE CYNICAL
INTERPRETATION
OF HISTORY*

In my long life I have never been bored – except at lectures, and especially those school lessons that produced a very painful numbing of the brain. I remember that the effect was particularly deadly in history and geography.

Perhaps it is forgivable, then, if many history teachers try to spice up their classes with a touch of cynicism. And it is understandable, though certainly not forgivable, if they go too far and make a cynical view of history the height of fashion.

The cynical interpretation states that, in history as well as more generally, greed is always in command – avarice, money-grubbing, gold, oil, and power. That, they say, is how it always has been and always will be, in despotic forms of rule but also in democracies, the only difference being that in the latter the hypocrisy is, if possible, even worse. I regard this theory as not only wrong but irresponsible, precisely because it has a ring of plausibility. I think there is an urgent need to combat it. For what we think about ourselves and our history is of some importance to us, important for our decisions and our actions. It is why I have chosen this topic today.

The cynical interpretation of history is the most recent of the three major fashions I should like to mention here. Nowadays it appears as a direct successor to the Marxist interpretation, which in turn became all the rage after the collapse of the nationalist or racist account of history.

* Lecture given at the University of Eichstätt in May 1991.

In Germany, the nationalist or racist interpretation of history flourished between the Napoleonic Wars and the collapse of Hitler's Reich. Being fashionable even before Hitler, it created an intellectual atmosphere, a view of the world, without which Hitler would not have been possible. It is partly Napoleon, partly Hegel whom we have to thank for this view of the world. History is seen as a struggle for dominance between nations and races in which the issue at stake is total extermination. According to this theory of history, the defeat of Hitler's Reich, for example, should have meant the total annihilation of the German people. It is well known that Hitler took every practical step at the end to bring about this theoretically predicted total annihilation of the German people. But despite his efforts, the prophecy happily proved to be false.

A theory worth taking seriously is discredited when a prediction does not come true, and something of the kind occurred with the highly fashionable nationalist interpretation of history. This certainly contributed to the fact that the Marxist interpretation of history became all the rage after the Hegelian and nationalist interpretations – by no means only in what was then Eastern Germany. As it is the intellectual collapse of the Marxist view of history that has recently led to the victory of the third, cynical fashion, I must start by examining that view a little more closely. Above all, I want to do this because the struggle against the Marxist interpretation of history has played an important role in my life.

The Marxist interpretation is known by the names 'materialist conception of history' and 'historical materialism', both of which go back to Marx and Engels. It is a reinterpretation of Hegel's philosophy of history, seeing history as consisting not of racial struggles but of class struggles. It has one aim: to furnish proof (scientific proof) that socialism (or communism – the words do not matter) *must* triumph as a historical inevitability.

This supposed proof can be found for the first time in the last three pages of Marx's book *The Poverty of Philosophy*, which originally appeared in French in 1847 as *Misère de la philosophie*. Here is the proof.

History is the history of class struggles. In our times (Marx was writing in 1847) this means struggles between the bourgeoisie, the exploiters, and the proletariat, the class of exploited producers. This struggle can end only with the victory of the producers, for if they become class-conscious and organized, they can bring production to a halt. 'All wheels stop when your strong arm wills it.' In other words, the producers hold the material power in their hands, even if they are not yet conscious of it. Besides, they make up the overwhelming majority. Their emancipation, their victory in the so-called 'social revolution', must therefore come to pass. This must end in the liquidation of the bourgeoisie, a process that takes place through a dictatorship of the victorious proletariat.

This ushers in a society made up of one single class, which is therefore a classless society of the producers. There is no longer a ruling class, and therefore – as soon as the bourgeoisie is liquidated – there are no rulers and no ruled. And the classless society brings with it the longed-for peace on earth, since all wars can only be class wars.

This, in a nutshell, is the ostensibly scientific proof of the 'historical necessity' with which socialism must arrive.

Already in 1847, on the penultimate page of *The Poverty of Philosophy*, Marx considered an objection to his account. Could it not be that after the fall of the old society there will be a new class domination culminating in a new political power? To this question of such evident importance, he answers with a single word: 'No.' He seems to assume that the class of producers will not itself divide; that there will not, as in the French Revolution, be a split between a new ruling class of Napoleonic dictators supported by their bureaucracy, police, and henchmen, on the one side, and *everyone else* on the other side. Marx did not envisage that.

The claim of Marxism to provide a scientific prediction of social revolution and the inevitable coming of socialism – just as a solar eclipse is predictable with the help of Newton's celestial mechanics – contains a terrible moral danger. I experienced this in my own life in the winter of 1918–1919, at the end of the First World War when I was sixteen and a half years old. When a youngster is taken in by the proof of the historical necessity of socialism, he feels a deep moral obligation to offer his help – even if he sees, as I did, that the communists often lie and employ morally reprehensible means. For if socialism *must* come about, it is obviously *criminal* to fight its coming. Indeed it is everyone's duty to further the coming of socialism, so that what must come will encounter as little resistance as possible. Since you are not strong enough as an individual, you have to go with the movement, with the Party, and give it your loyal support, even if this means you support or at least swallow things you find morally repulsive. This is a mechanism that must lead to personal depravity. You swallow more and more intellectual trickery, excuses and lies. And once you go beyond a certain threshold, you are presumably prepared to accept anything. That is the road to political terrorism, to crime.

I myself escaped this mechanism after eight weeks or so, when I rejected Marxism once and for all shortly before my seventeenth birthday. Feeling affected by the death of some young comrades who had been shot by the police at a demonstration, I asked myself: 'Do you really *know* that this supposedly scientific proof holds water? Have you critically tested it in any real way? Can you take responsibility for encouraging other young people to put their lives on the line?'

I found that a clear 'No' was the only honest answer to these questions. I had not really critically tested the Marxist proof. I had partly let myself become dependent upon the approval of others, who depended upon others (including myself) in their turn – a mutual insurance in which all partners are intellectually bankrupt and (unconsciously) tempt one another into falsehood. It was a state I recognized in myself, and it evidently had the party leaders most emphatically in its grip.

Everything turned upon the Marxist proof of the coming of a classless society, I learnt. But this broke down at the very point where Marx had seen and denied the possibility of a counter-argument. Clearly it is the party leaders who, with the party's help, form the beginnings of a 'new class' and thereby negate Marx's hopes. This 'new ruling class' deceives and mistrusts its future subjects, yet demands their trust. Already before victory and dictatorship, the leaders were rulers who expelled from the party anyone who posed awkward questions. (They could not yet kill such people.) This was their way of dealing with questions. This was the source of party discipline.

I had the great and undeserved good fortune to see all this in time. On my seventeenth birthday I turned my back on Marxism for good. What would have become of me if I had gone along with it any longer? Even a brave and determined dissident like Sakharov was for a long time sufficiently captivated by the Marxist proof to press into the hands first of Stalin (via his henchman Beria), and then of Khrushchev, the most terrible weapons of mass destruction ever invented. Even in its weaker version, Sakharov's superbomb was designed to be 'several thousand times more powerful than the bomb dropped on Hiroshima'.[1]

I myself later met important scientists who believed in Marx's proof and were members of the Communist Party. I am proud that I was able to persuade one of the greatest to leave. He was the great biologist J.B.S. Haldane.

On the occasion of Stalin's death, Sakharov excused Stalin's crimes as humanistic deeds, on the grounds that such things were unavoidable in (what he saw as) the social revolution of decisive importance for humanity. But fortunately it became clear to me very early on that one should sacrifice only oneself, and not anyone else, for one's ideals.

Although Marx's proof was intended to show the inevitability of the coming of socialism and peace on earth, there are other features in the Marxist view of history that may well be described as vulgar-Marxist. Let us briefly summarize them. Everyone who does not struggle for socialism is motivated by self-interest and nothing else. If people do not admit this, they are just swindlers and hypocrites – indeed, criminals in a big way. For if they try to delay the coming of socialism, they bear the guilt for all the human sacrifices that will have to be made for the revolution. It is resistance to the unstoppable revolution that forces it to act violently. It is the greed of such criminals that forces revolutionaries to shed blood.

Now I come to the third great fashion in the interpretation of history.

It is clear that if the coming of socialism is dropped from Marxist theory, a cynical view of history directly follows. No new ideas are needed – or at most, only the pessimistic idea that things always have been and always will be so, that hunger, forced exile, war, and poverty will play the major role even in a society of real abundance, because the social world is ruled by people greedy for power, gold, and oil, and by the unscrupulous weapons industry.

Marxism, and therefore cynicism as well, teach that everything is of course worst in the wealthiest country of all, the United States of America. This is how anti-Americanism arises in other countries, especially those not quite as rich.

This closes my brief sketch of the ultramodern cynical view of history and its two dangerously influential predecessors. Now I turn abruptly to some of my own views. How abruptly, you will see from my next statement, which I could use as the title for the second half of my remarks. This is: *I am an optimist.*

I am an optimist who has no knowledge of the future and therefore makes no predictions. We must make a very clear division between the present, which we can and should judge, and the wide-open future, which we are able to influence. We therefore have a moral duty to face the future quite differently from how we would if it were just a continuation of the past and present. The open future contains unforeseeable and morally quite different possibilities. So our basic attitude should not be 'What will happen?' but 'What should we do to make the world a little better – even if we know that once we have done it, future generations might make everything worse again?'

The second half of my talk, then, also deals with two questions: *my optimism about the present*; and *my activism with regard to the future.*

Let me say straight away that it was my first trip to the United States in 1950 that made an optimist of me again. Since then I have been to America twenty or maybe twenty-five times, and each time I have been more deeply impressed. That first trip tore me for ever out of a depression caused by the overwhelming influence of Marxism in postwar Europe. My book *The Open Society and Its Enemies*, which I began in 1938 after Hitler marched into Austria, had finally been published in 1945. But although it sold well and was favourably reviewed, it seemed impossible to do anything about the triumph of Marxism.

Here I should explain the main components of my optimism.

1   I repeat that my optimism refers exclusively to the present, not to the future. I do not think there is such a thing as a law of progress. There is not even one in science or technology. Progress cannot even be described as likely.

2   I claim that we in the West now live in the best social world there has ever been – despite the high treason of most intellectuals, who preach a new pessimistic religion according to which we live in a moral hell and are perishing from physical and moral pollution.

3   I argue that this pessimistic religion is a blatant lie, and – to come straight to one of my main points – that never before has there been a society as enthusiastic for reform as our own.

4   This enthusiasm for reform is the result of a new ethical willing- ness to make sacrifices, a willingness that was already apparent (on both sides) in the two world wars. In the Seven Years' War, Friedrich II still had to force his men to look death in the face. His rallying-cry is well known: 'You curs, do you want to live for ever?' But then it turned out that an appeal to ethical values is enough: to duty and fatherland in Germany, to fatherland, free- dom, and peace in the West; and on both sides to comradeship.

As I have already indicated from my own experience, I think the power of communism lies in its ethical appeal; and the same is true of the peace movement. I think also that many terrorists originally responded to an ethical appeal, which caught them, however, in that inner duplicity I have already mentioned.

Bertrand Russell, to whom I felt very close for many years until, as an old man, he fell under the sway of a communist secretary, wrote that the problem of our time is that our development has been too fast intellectually and too slow morally, so that when we discovered nuclear physics we did not achieve in time the necessary moral principles. In other words, according to Russell we are too clever – but morally, we are too bad. Many people, including many cynics, shared Russell's view. I believe the exact opposite. I believe that we are too good and too stupid. We are too easily swayed by theories that appeal directly or indirectly to our moral sense, and our attitude to these theories is not sufficiently critical. We are not intellectually mature enough for them, and become their obliging victims, ready to make sacrifices of ourselves.

I would summarize as follows the positive side of my optimism. We live in a simply wonderful world, and here in the West we have created the best social system there has ever been. We are constantly trying to improve it, to reform it – which is far from easy. Many reforms that look promising turn out to be misconceived. For it is very important to realize that the consequences of our social and political actions are often quite different from what we intended and were able to foresee. Nevertheless, we have achieved far more than many of us (myself, for example) ever hoped.

The prevailing ideology, which sees us living in a morally evil world, is a blatant lie. As it spreads, it discourages many young people and makes them despondent – at an age when they may not be able to live at all without some hope to support them. To repeat: I am not an optimist regarding the future. For the future is open. There is no historical law of progress. We do not know what tomorrow will be like. There are billions of possibilities, good and bad, that no one can foresee. I reject the prophetic goal-setting of the three interpretations of history, and I maintain that on moral grounds we should not put *anything* in their place. It is wrong even to try to extrapolate from history – for example, by inferring from present trends what will happen tomorrow. To see history as an at least partly predictable current is to build a theory out of an image or metaphor.

The only right way to proceed is to consider the past as completely different from the future. We should judge past facts historically and morally, in order to learn what is possible and what is morally right. We should not try at all to derive trends and directions from the past in order to make predictions about the future. For the future is open. Anything can happen. At this moment, there are thousands of Sakharov's superbombs in the Soviet Union, and there are certainly plenty of megalomaniacs who would be happy to use them. Mankind *may* be wiped out tomorrow. But there are also great hopes; there are countless possibilities for a future that will be far better than the present.

Unfortunately, this way of looking at the future does not seem easy to grasp. Some intellectuals are simply incapable of making this distinction between the future and the past and present – intellectuals who have learnt from Marxism to require some wise man to point the way into the future. More than once I have been told that my optimism must be at least a *disguised* pointer, because there are no optimists about the present who are not also optimists about the future.

But *all that my optimism about the present can offer for the future is hope.* It can give us hope and incentive; for we have succeeded in making a lot of things better, and similar success is not impossible in the future. Since maids were released from thraldom in the 1920s, for example, there has been virtually no servitude in the West. We can be proud of the fact that, in this sense at least, the West is free.

As far as the future is concerned, we should not seek to prophesy but simply try to act in a way that is morally right and responsible. This means we have a duty to learn to see the present correctly, not through the tinted spectacles of an ideology. We can learn from reality what it is *possible* to achieve. But if we see reality through the lens of one of those three ideological conceptions of history, we violate our duty to learn.

The future is open, and we have a responsibility to do our best to make the future still better than the present. But this responsibility presupposes freedom. In a despotic system we are slaves, and *slaves are not fully responsible for what they do.* This brings me to my final main thesis.

Political freedom – *freedom from despotism* – is the most important of all political values. And we must always be prepared to struggle for political freedom. It can always be lost. We should never sit back and assume that our freedom is secure.

Under despotic rule, all are in danger of betraying mankind and thus of losing their humanity, of becoming dehumanized. Even someone like Andrei Sakharov (whose later admirable behaviour showed he had the courage to resist despotism), even he, as a young man, could behave like a sadistic criminal. Not only did he, as I showed, press the most terrible weapons of mass destruction into the blood-stained hands of Stalin's henchman, the sadist Beria; he developed a still more terrible plan for their use by the Russian Navy. A high-ranking officer rejected this plan, because it conflicted with his combat morality, and Sakharov writes that he felt ashamed of himself. All this happened because he was blinded by that crazy and depraved Marxist ideology and therefore believed in the mission of Stalin the great humanist – which is how he saw him at the time. In this climate of despotism, Sakharov temporarily became a really mad beast – temporarily, but for long enough to prepare the greatest conceivable disaster, to hang a sword of Damocles over every living creature.

Despotism robs us of our humanity, for it robs us of our responsibility as human beings. Someone who seeks to follow his conscience then finds himself faced with impossibilities: insoluble conflicts, such as that between his duties to his family and his duty to stand by the persecuted, or at least his duty not to collaborate in their persecution. He must have great courage not to confuse his true duties to himself with a false so-called duty to the despots standing over him, a duty that Sakharov had promised Khrushchev he would fulfil and that he later used in his defence – just as the German war criminals did.

How despotism destroys the human sense of duty and responsibility, together with the people who try to fulfil them, may be seen from the unforgettable example of the White Rose in Munich, that close circle of students and one teacher who in the winter of 1942–43 put up posters calling for resistance to Hitler's war. Hans Scholl and his sister Sophie were executed along with Christoph Probst on 22 February 1943; Alexander Schmorell and Professor Kurt Huber on 13 July 1943; Willi Graf on 12 October 1943. Hans Scholl was 24 years old and Sophie 21; the other students were the same age. Some of their comrades are still alive today.

Heroes who can be examples to us have become a rarity in our generation. Those people were heroes: they initiated a struggle that was almost hopeless for them, in the hope that others would take it over. And they are examples: they fought for freedom and responsibility and for their and our humanity. The monstrous inhuman force of despotism reduced them to silence. We should not forget them. And we must speak and act for them.

Political freedom is a prerequisite of our personal responsibility, our humanity. Any attempt to take a step towards a better world, a better future, must be guided by the *basic value of freedom.*

I find it tragic that Europe has nearly always concentrated only on the failed example of the French Revolution (failed until de Gaulle set up the Fifth Republic, at least), whereas little attention is paid (at least at school) to the great and nearly always misunderstood example of the American Revolution. For America furnished proof that the idea of personal freedom, which Solon of Athens first tried to implement and Kant extensively analysed, is not a Utopian dream. The American example has shown that a form of government dedicated to freedom is not only possible but capable of overcoming the greatest difficulties. Above all, it is a form of government based upon the *avoidance of despotism* – not least the despotism of a majority of the people – through the division and distribution of power and through reciprocal checks and balances among the powers so divided. This idea has inspired all other democracies, including the basic law of Germany's democracy.

But America had to go through difficult times. It has been going through them ever since the Revolution and War of Independence, and despite its great successes it has not yet seen the end of them. The struggle for freedom goes on.

The great idea of the freedom of every individual, which inspired the American Revolution, stood in the sharpest contrast to the institution of slavery inherited from pre-revolutionary times, especially from the Spanish, which had been deeply rooted in the Southern States for more than a hundred years. The United States split in two over the issue, when the South launched a preventive war against the North. It was certainly the most terrible war there had yet been, a civil war in which friends and members of the same family confronted each other. It seemed to many that America's road to freedom would prove as unsuccessful as France's. But despite the heaviest sacrifices on both sides (600,000 dead, one of them President Abraham Lincoln), the South's initially successful attack was repulsed and eventually overwhelmed. The slaves were freed, but a huge problem remained of how to integrate the descendants of the former negro slaves; how to overcome a cruel, centuries-old institution which, because of differences in skin colour, was not so easily forgotten.

I have yet to see a German historical work in which this situation has been even moderately accurately described and evaluated.

One of the strongest impressions in my life comes from my witnessing, between 1950 and 1989, the various attempts made by U.S. governments to help the former slaves to become citizens with equal rights. I shall just mention one episode. In 1956 I was a guest at the University of Atlanta, in the heart of the former Southern States. The University then had only black students, and white professors were in a minority. Once I asked the president, a distinguished black scholar, how and when this great and wonderful institution had come to be founded. To my astonishment, I learnt that this black university in the Deep South originated six years after the Civil War, through the amalgamation of a number of Negro Colleges – I think it was eight – that had been founded by all the Christian Churches as places where white and black clergy and teachers worked alongside one another.

I leave it up to you to ponder this story, and to compare it with an entry in *Meyers Enzyklopädisches Lexicon* which says about the end of the Civil War: 'Slavery, on the other hand, which had been the cause of the war, underwent only the appearance of a solution.' This seems to me quite wrong, as does much else in the article in question, and I wonder what genuine solution the author would have proposed. Anyway, the history of the University of Atlanta made a strong impression on me, as did many other endeavours that I have seen with my own eyes.

I have been in many countries, but nowhere have I breathed as freely as in the United States of America. Nowhere have I found so much idealism coupled with tolerance and a desire to help and learn – such an active, practical idealism, such a great willingness to help. Later I was also in American universities where the integration of blacks had been a complete success, so that skin colour no longer seemed to play any role at all.

I say all this in perfect awareness that it may not receive an enthusiastic reception. Three years ago at a congress in Hanover, I gave a lecture in defence of America because it had been attacked in a number of other lectures. There was a veritable hue and cry, and my words were accompanied by a chorus of whistles. I welcomed this as a sign that my audience was not bored. And I was happy because I could imagine – or could talk myself into believing – that I was taking up the cudgels for freedom and toleration.

Note

1 I am quoting from Andrei Sakharov, *Memoirs*, Hutchinson, London, 1990, p. 218.

11

'WAGING WARS FOR PEACE'*

Spiegel Herr Popper, the collapse of the Soviet Union has fulfilled a prophecy you made as much as half a century ago. Is this the triumph of critical rationalism over the enemies of the open society?

Popper I made no such prophecies, because I am of the view that no prophecies should be made. I think it is a completely wrong attitude to judge intellectuals by whether they make good prophecies.
The philosophy of history in Germany, at least since Hegel, has always thought it must somehow be prophetic. I think this is wrong. One learns from history, but history ends here and now. Our attitude to the future must be quite different from one of trying to extrapolate from history and, as it were, following the paths of history through into the future.

Spiegel Very well, if it was not a prophecy, you did at least expect liberal democracy to be victorious over various forms of despotism.

Popper Our attitude to the future must be: we are responsible now for what happens in the future. The past is something already given. We can no longer do anything about it, even if we are in another sense responsible for the past: that is, held responsible for what we have done. But for the future we are morally responsible here and now: we must do the best we can without any ideological lenses – even when the prospects are not too bright. The best is quite definitely what is least violent, what reduces suffering, unnecessary suffering.

Spiegel Is it not true that, already in Lenin's time, Left Communists

* Interview first published in *Der Spiegel*, April 1992, reprinted with the kind permission of Spiegel Verlag.

complained that the state ideology established in Russia with a single-party dictatorship had little in common with the original theories of Karl Marx, who wagered on a proletarian revolution in the industrialized West?

Popper I would say the following to that. The communist mania – and you find this already in Marx – is essentially a view of the so-called capitalist world as diabolic. What Marx called capitalism has never existed on earth, nor anything like it.

Spiegel Do you mean that there was never such a thing as Manchester liberalism with its terrible working conditions?

Popper Of course those were terribly hard times for the workers, but also for other people. Marx was mainly interested in the workers. As a simple historical fact, things have kept getting better for them since that time, whereas Marx claimed that they would keep going downhill and must keep going downhill.

Spiegel Do you mean his theory of absolute impoverishment?

Popper Yes. And because the impoverishment theory did not prove true, the impoverishment was transposed to the colonies – to what is nowadays called the Third World ...

Spiegel The so-called theory of imperialism.

Popper A typical intellectual's formula and, of course, complete nonsense. For industrialization cannot be the same as impoverishment – that is as clear as anything can be. Things kept getting better for the colonies too.

So what was so-called capitalism? It was industrialization and mass production. And mass production means that a lot is produced, so that very many people get something. For mass production requires a large market and therefore a lot of buyers. Marx compared capitalism to hell. And hell has existed on earth just as little as Dante's Inferno. *Lasciate ogni speranza* ('Abandon all hope') that is a conception of Dante's Inferno that Marx explicitly attributed to capitalism. And if capitalism necessarily leads to impoverishment, then the only possible way out is a social revolution.

I am very critical of our contemporary society. A lot of things could be improved in it. But our liberal social order is the best and justest there has ever been on earth. It arose through evolution from *the one that Marx knew*.

Spiegel Is anything at all left of the ethical appeal of Marx's critique of capitalism as socially unjust? Has the gulf between rich and poor actually narrowed on a world scale?

Popper The ethical appeal has existed in various forms since the Middle Ages. Among Christian thinkers, as well as among Enlightenment thinkers, the ethical appeal was paramount. And those opposed to this ethical appeal were essentially the Romantics.

Spiegel When you mention the Enlightenment, are you mainly thinking of Kant's call for a just civil constitution to spread throughout the world, as the highest duty of humanity? And is Hegel the chief Romantic for you?

Popper Quite right. The Romantic alternative was more or less that nothing can work without war and violence; that was how Hegel applied his experience of history. But if you consistently apply the past experiences of military conflict to our future, then there is really no hope left. For our weapons can now annihilate us. The omnicidal bath of atomic radiation has taken the place of the bloodbath of steel that seemed so invigorating to our Romantic forebears.

Spiegel What caused the collapse in Eastern Europe? Was it the economic drain of the arms race, or an intellectual bankruptcy, or doubt about their mission?

Popper A lot of things were involved: for example, that Hungary opened its borders for East Germans fleeing the GDR; or that Gorbachev instructed the Soviet Politburo to make an attempt at reform. But the economic reform was of absolutely no avail. The economy cannot be reformed from above. Then there was the intellectual desolation. All that was left of Marxism were empty words and a single substantive formula: 'Liquidate capitalism!' – the nonexistent diabolical capitalism. Khrushchev tried to translate that into reality.

Spiegel Are you thinking of the poker game in 1962 when Soviet missiles were deployed in Fidel Castro's Cuba?

Popper Khrushchev had planned a devastating assault on the USA. He pulled back only when the Americans were ready to attack. The nuclear physicist Andrei Sakharov wrote in his *Memoirs* that even in a 'clean version' his Big Bomb would still be several thousand times more powerful than the Hiroshima bomb. Thirty-six of those bombs had already arrived in Cuba. And if Sakharov's 'several' means only three, that makes 108,000 Hiroshima bombs. You just have to try to imagine it. In his farewell speech, Gorbachev said there exist some 30,000 of these bombs.

The Cuban crisis revealed what Marxism was capable of doing to achieve its aims: it was capable of trying to destroy capitalism with nuclear weapons. This should never be forgotten. Not only America would have gone under in such an attack; the whole world would have perished in a bath of radiation – even if it took a few terrible years.

Spiegel What does the world owe the perestroika reformer Gorbachev, who has now been swallowed up by his own reforms?

Popper A great deal. Gorbachev started to look at America in a way that Soviet rulers had not done before. He went there more than once and enjoyed being fêted. Then he came up with an interesting un-Marxist formulation: I want the Soviet Union to become a normal country. That was an approximation to our idea of the rule of law. Gorbachev wanted to make the Soviet Union normal. We owe this completely new idea to him. That the Soviet Union had not previously been a normal country, we can see most clearly from Sakharov's *Memoirs*.

Spiegel The collapse of Soviet Communism and the end of the bipolar system have not made the world a safer place. Everywhere we have to face the return of nationalist demons, loosely controlled nuclear weapons, and the migration of people stricken by poverty. Are these the new enemies of liberal democracy?

Popper Our first objective today must be peace. It is very hard to achieve in a world such as ours, where Saddam Hussein and other dictators like him exist. We should not shrink from waging war for peace. In present conditions that is unavoidable. It is sad, but we have to do it if we want to save our world. Resolve is crucially important here.

Spiegel War to stop the further spread of weapons of mass destruction?

Popper At the moment, nothing is more important than to prevent the spread of these lunatic bombs, which are already being traded on the black market. The states of the civilized world that have not gone mad must work together on this. For I repeat: just one Sakharov bomb is several thousand times more powerful than the Hiroshima bomb. This means that, in any densely populated country, the detonation of just one bomb would cause millions of deaths, quite apart from the victims of radiation who would die of the effects over a number of years. We must not get used to such things. Here we must take action.

Spiegel   Should the Americans act against Saddam again if it looks as if he is making bombs?

Popper   Not only against Saddam. There should be a kind of task force of the civilized world for such cases. To be pacifist in the out-moded sense would be madness. We must wage wars for peace – obviously in the least terrible form. Since it is a question of force, force must be used to stop the bomb being used.

Spiegel   Now you are talking almost like Pentagon strategists who wish for a new world order against a background of *pax Americana* that would also stall economic competition from Japan and Europe.

Popper   I think it is criminal to talk like that. The need to prevent nuclear war cannot be confused with economic questions. We should try to cooperate so actively in this *pax Americana* that it becomes a *pax civilitatis*. This is simply what the situation requires. It is not a minor issue but the survival of mankind that is at stake.

Spiegel   During his trip to Germany, Gorbachev complained that if the West had given massive aid, the August putsch in Moscow would not have happened and he would not have fallen in its aftermath. Should the West do more for Boris Yeltsin, so that Russia does not sink into a still worse despotism?

Popper   I think we should help. But Gorbachev has no right to com-plain. We owe him a lot, but he went on arming. The condition for our aid should be that Russia works together with us, the civilized countries, to bring these terrible weapons under effective control. But the Russian military has to be involved too.

Spiegel   You are convinced that we live in the best and justest society there has ever been. But this liberal democracy has no convincing solutions to offer against widespread hunger in the Third World or the destruction of the environment.

Popper   We are more than able to feed the whole world. The eco-nomic problem has been solved – by technologists, not by economists.

Spiegel   But you can hardly dispute that there is mass poverty in large parts of the Third World.

Popper   No. But that is mainly due to the political stupidity of lead-ers in the various countries where there is mass hunger. We freed them too quickly and in too crude a way. They have yet to become states based on the rule of law. The same would happen if you left a kindergarten to its own devices.

Spiegel Are economic conflicts nowadays the continuation of war by other means? Europe and the USA are afraid they are losing the microchip war against the Japanese.

Popper These problems should not be taken seriously, and they should not be discussed in this way. It is what I have called the cynical view of history: intellectuals want to be clever instead of offering help. The Japanese are really civilized. You can talk to them. But time and again we are up against stupidity, both here and of course in Japan too.

Spiegel Stupidity? Do you mean strategies of economic conquest?

Popper Yes. Japan has big problems: it is overpopulated. But that can be discussed later. Unfortunately there are always journalists who misunderstand these things and are looking for a sensation. We have enough sensations already.

Spiegel But it has not simply been invented by journalists. The current 'Don't buy Japanese goods!' campaign in the USA suggests a deep sense of confrontation.

Popper Such a confrontation is nonsense. The whole thing is unimportant. At present Japan is not at all imperialistic. True, it has the industry and the potential to manufacture nuclear weapons at any time. But the Japanese know what that would mean.

In my view, theoretical economics has ground to a kind of intellectual halt; it has become bogged down in current problems. But the problems can all be solved. No millionaire has yet died of riches. And compared with the prewar world, you in Germany are all millionaires now.

Spiegel But overuse of the wealth of resources is evidently helping to blight our planet. Keyword: ozone hole.

Popper But such things are not known yet. Ozone holes may have existed for millions of years. It is possible they have no connection with anything modern.

Spiegel Renowned scientists see things differently. They think there really is a connection between chlorine concentrations and destruction of the ozone layer.

Popper   Renowned scientists are not always right. I am not saying they are wrong – only that we often know less than we think.

Spiegel   These are questions you usually argue about with the Greens, and from time to time they really let fly at you. Why is that?

Popper   Because of their really crazy hostility to science and technology. There is an anti-rationalist kernel in the Greens that leads to the exact opposite of what they are supposed to want. They also want power themselves, and are as hypocritical as they claim their opponents to be.

Environmental disasters are largely due to the population explosion, which we must solve ethically. Really, only children who are wanted should come into the world.

Spiegel   How do you think that can be achieved – through government directives, as in China?

Popper   Not through government directives but through education. Unwanted children are at risk, and I mean morally. People who do not want them should have the means not to have them. The means exist already – I am thinking of the abortion pill.

Spiegel   The Catholic Church and the Pope are not on your side there.

Popper   The Church and the Pope will give way, especially if convincing ethical reasons are given. I am thinking of things like rape, or the birth of children infected with AIDS, or those who, in some countries, come into the world with practically no chances in life. It is a crime not to help such children by stopping them being born. The Church must and will give way on this; it is just a matter of time.

Spiegel   Herr Popper, we should now like to talk about a few questions concerning Germany. One of the changes to the balance of power in Europe is the stronger, reunified Germany. Is there any reason why neighbouring countries should feel concerned?

Popper   Of course there is. But the present situation in Germany – political and moral – is much better than one might have hoped. This says something about the basic rationality of human beings. But we do not know what lies ahead. It is a paradoxical thing about human well-being that, while it is based on vigilance against a host of dangers, it also undermines that vigilance. Freedom easily comes to be taken for granted – which means that one can again fall victim to a dictator. There have already been some possible signs of this in Austria.

Spiegel   You can hardly say that, really. Presumably you are thinking of Jörg Haider, the spokesman of the right-wing Freedom Party?

Popper   Yes. Young people there are keen on Haider. It has to do with the stupidity of their education. Haider's ideal is Hitler. He would like to do what Hitler did.

Spiegel   He is not really saying that.

Popper   He says it clearly enough to be heard. He says it for those who want to hear.

Spiegel   In sixty years Germany has lived through two totalitarian systems. Right now we are faced with the problem of integrating the SED-Stasi state, where there was no rule of law. How can political guilt be measured? Can we in the West sit in moral judgement?

Popper   We can certainly sit in moral judgement on the leading group of the former GDR, on those who were really responsible. I think that the attempts to make Honecker stand trial are very important.

Spiegel   So you are not in favour of a widescale reckoning in a blaze of public denunciations, but only of the trial of some exemplary cases?

Popper   It is extremely important that we manage with the least possible vengeance and similar abominations such as those committed in the former GDR.

Spiegel   And without bigotry.

Popper   Without bigotry too. The court must proceed with the utmost caution. The trial should deal only with the crimes of the former leaders – a hundred and fifty people at the most. That much should be done, but it is simply not possible to go any further – apart from anything else, it would trivialize things.

Spiegel   And would you spare the collaborators because people are not heroes and, in a totalitarian society, they do what has to be done to lead a reasonably normal life?

Popper   That is right. Too much should not be done to those who collaborated. Most of them were afraid. That is the method of terrorism – to frighten people. But there is some point at which heroism begins for everyone – the point when one is being forced actually to commit base and evil deeds. Then one does have to be a hero and to resist.

Spiegel   The neo-conservative philosopher Francis Fukuyama, who is currently in fashion in America, thinks that the ending of ideological conflicts and the worldwide spread of liberal democracy have brought 'the end of history'. The victory of democracy is supposed to have concluded the ideological evolution of humanity.

Popper Those are just silly phrases. There is no philosophical miracle. Marx too said that with the 'social revolution' the end of history would be nigh, because history is only the history of class struggle.

Spiegel Behind Fukuyama can be seen someone you do not greatly appreciate: namely, Hegel and his theory of the historical process as a series of contradictions that finally reaches its goal with the realization of freedom on earth.

Popper Of course. Hegel would say 'yes' to that, because he saw history as a history of power. That is also largely what it was. Our history books never took the development of humanity as their main theme, but only the history of power.

Of course, we do need an end of history – that is, an ending of the history of power. This has become necessary because of nuclear weapons. It was always morally necessary, but now the excess of weapons has made it necessary for survival.

Spiegel Already before Hiroshima, you wrote that man will one day disappear from the face of the earth.

Popper Why not? There are incalculable dangers. Just as all of us die, mankind too will probably die. Perhaps we will one day perish along with the solar system. But there is no point in talking, or even thinking, about such things. More likely is what I predicted long before AIDS – that some microbe will polish us off. That could happen very quickly. Any time. But there could still be many thousands of years to go until then.

Spiegel To repeat, then: there is no law of progress, no logical endpoint?

Popper Nothing like that. What there really is, is our enormous responsibility not to be cruel. For example, it is simply incomprehensible how we can allow children with AIDS to come into the world. For the Churches, too, the first attitude to life must be: no cruelty.

Spiegel Herr Popper, you are nearly ninety years of age and have always described yourself as an optimist through and through. But this interview has struck some very pessimistic notes. Has new knowledge come in the evening of life?

Popper   Optimism is a duty. One must focus on the things that need to be done and for which one is responsible. What I have said in this interview is meant to make you and others vigilant. We must live so that our grandchildren have a better life than ours – and not just in an economic sense.

Spiegel   Herr Popper, we thank you for this interview.

12

THE COLLAPSE OF COMMUNISM: UNDERSTANDING THE PAST AND INFLUENCING THE FUTURE*

As you will have surmised from the title of my lecture, I am an opponent of Marxism. My lecture will be devoted to the Marxist attack upon our Western civilization, an attack that began with Lenin's and Trotsky's Revolution of October 1917 and of whose breakdown we meeting here today are the living witnesses.

Few of us here will be old enough to remember personally the beginning of all our troubles; but I am one of the few alive who vividly recall 28 June 1914, the day on which the Archduke Franz Ferdinand of Austria was assassinated in Sarajevo. I can still hear the voice of the newspaper boy announcing that the assassin was a Serb ('*Der Täter ein Serbe!*'). And I vividly remember the outbreak of the First World War on 28 July 1914 (my twelfth birthday). I learnt of the war in a letter from my father, and also from the large placard on which was printed a manifesto from Emperor Franz Joseph 'To My Peoples'. I still remember the day in 1916 when I realized that Austria and Germany were going to lose the war they had started; I remember the days in March 1917 when a democratic revolution started in Russia; I remember Lenin's putsch against the Kerensky government and the beginning of civil war in Russia; the peace treaty of Brest-Litovsk between Germany and the Russia of Lenin and Trotsky, in March 1918; and the collapse of the Austrian and German empires, which ended the war, in October 1918. These events were among the most important that I still vividly remember

* Lecture given in English on 6 March 1992 in Seville within the framework of Expo '92.

and, as I can now see, led all mankind close to its complete destruction.

In a brief lecture I must, of course, radically oversimplify. I shall have to paint my historical portraits with a broad brush and in the crudest of colours.

Before the First World War, industrialization in Western Europe, Germany, and North America might well have led to the victory of a truly liberal society. In fact, these parts of the world did know both liberty and great economic success; open frontiers, no need for passports, decreasing criminality and violence, growing literacy, and rising wages and prosperity. Thanks to technological advances, there was even some improvement in the still horribly hard conditions of manual work. The First World War, started by Germany and Austria, destroyed all this and showed that the old forms of government could no longer be trusted. We are still faced with the same problem.

At the end of the First World War, the defeated powers – Germany, Austria, Turkey – were overthrown from outside. But there was also a revolution, especially in Austria, partly under the influence of the Russian Revolution. Of the victorious powers, France and Italy were also deeply shaken. Only Great Britain and the United States resumed their prewar steps towards liberal reform, though only after the defeat of a general strike in England that was an attempt to start a revolution, partly influenced by Russia.

The example of the two English-speaking countries undoubtedly had a stabilizing effect, in spite of the Great Bank Crash and the Great Depression. England in 1935, in spite of unemployment and the Hitler threat, was the happiest industrial nation in Europe I have seen in the whole of my life: every manual worker, every bus conductor and taxi driver, and every police constable, was a perfect gentleman. But the Marxist victory in Russia, and the enormous amounts spent by the Communists on propaganda and organization of the World Revolution, had led everywhere in the West to a sharp polarization between Left and Right. First in Italy under Mussolini, this polarization led to fascism, soon to be copied by fascist movements in other European countries, especially Germany and Austria, and to an endemic civil war – very one-sided, since it consisted mainly of terrorists of the Right.

So the following situation emerged. In the East, especially in the Soviet Union, Marxism was ruling ruthlessly, with dictatorial powers based upon a powerful ideology and an unlimited arsenal of lies. In the West – under the influence of Marxist parties, of propaganda and fascination with Russia's might, and the hope of a socialist society –

there was constantly a serious threat of violence (but little real violence) from strong powers on the Left, evoking real counter-violence from the Right and thus strengthening the fascists. Germany, Austria, and the southern part of Europe succumbed to fascism under the sharpened polarization between Left and Right, which culminated in the terrible civil war in Spain, conducted in part as an experiment in modern warfare by the Soviets and the German Nazis. Fascist parties developed even in France and Great Britain. But democracy maintained itself there and in the smaller countries of Northern Europe.

In this situation preceding Hitler's war against the West, almost all the wise men, almost all the intellectuals, declared that democracy was just a passing phase in human history and prophesied its impending disappearance. Incidentally, I started my book on the open society with an attack upon these people and the mischievous fashion of historical prophecy.

Then Hitler started the Second World War, and lost it, thanks to one man: Winston Churchill. It is thanks to him that a coalition of the Western democracies and Russia was cemented that was ultimately able to beat Hitler and his allies. Yet as one of the consequences, the powers of the Left in the Left–Right polarization within the democracies became stronger than ever before. Although fascism was beaten everywhere, owing to Hitler's and Mussolini's defeat, there arose an even more threatening Cold War between East and West, with the East more unified than ever under the iron fist of Communist dictatorship, and the Western democracies still internally split and undermined. Here the Left was egged on and supported by the Soviets, who also stirred up the Middle East and indeed the world against the so-called capitalist countries of the West.

In spite of all that, the free democracies, the open societies of the West, did win. It was not they who broke under their colossal internal strains – strains that they always openly discussed. It was the highly integrated and totally united Communist dictatorship of East Germany that broke first, and that carried with it the iron fist of the united Soviet Empire.

Ladies and gentlemen, please consider the immense strains that the democracies were capable of enduring. I would say that they were the greatest ever endured by *any* political power group. And this power group was a very loose collection of democratic nations, each torn by forces from inside and threatened – even attacked – by overwhelming forces from outside that sharpened those inner tensions, each having great problems to solve that were its very own and not even understood by its closest allies. Each was 'a house divided against itself' (Mark iii: 25), and each was a house threatened by tremendous forces from outside. But these houses, these free societies, could and did stand; they were open societies.

The closed, tightly bound and united house held together by iron chains – this was the one that broke and splintered into bits.

So the open societies have won, and the Soviet empire has lost. Fortunately, it has lost without a shot having been fired by us or by them – at least so far. Unfortunately, there was (and still is) internal bloodshed among our late enemies who are now being helped by us in their misery, the misery that Marxism has brought them, even though we ourselves are in the midst of an economic crisis at least in part brought upon us by them.

My theory of these great and important events that we have witnessed since 1989, and which are far from concluded, my theory of the disease that led to the death of Marxism, can be summed up in the formula:

Marxism died of Marxism.

Or to be more explicit: Marxist power died of the barrenness of Marxist theory. Marxist theory, Marxist ideology, was perhaps quite clever, but it contradicted the facts of history and social life: it was an utterly false theory, and an utterly pretentious theory. And its many falsities, its many theoretical failures, were papered over with countless little lies, and with big lies. Lying, supported by brutal authority and violence, soon became the standard intellectual currency of the Communist dictatorial class inside Russia, and of the aspiring class of hopeful dictators outside Russia. The universe of lies contracted into an intellectual black hole. As you know, a black hole has the unlimited power to devour and to destroy everything, turning it into nothing. The difference between lying and speaking the truth disappeared. The intellectual emptiness in the end devoured itself: so Marxism has died of Marxism – in fact it did so long ago. But millions of Marxists East and West will, I fear, continue with it as they did before, whatever may have happened in the real world: facts can be ignored, or they can be explained away.

Here ends the introductory part of my lecture – a broad and very rough historical survey. The rest of my lecture is divided into two parts. The first will give a brief outline and critique of Marxism; and the second will attempt to show how the new situation might be used for an improvement of our lives by way of a *political reform* of our democracies: a reform not so much of our institutions as of our outlook.

However, since the introduction was perhaps a little too abstract, I felt that I should insert here something autobiographical, rather than continue throughout in the same abstract style, which might tire you before I even come to my brief exposition and critique of Marxist theory. So I decided to make my lecture more lively by reporting a piece of my own early history: how I was converted to Marxism – or very nearly converted; how it came about that I turned into a lifelong opponent of Marxism, just before my seventeenth birthday on 28 July 1919.

My parents were strong pacifists even before the First World War, and my father was a liberal, a very scholarly lawyer influenced by Immanuel Kant, Wilhelm von Humboldt, and John Stuart Mill. I was fourteen or fifteen when, during the war, I was struck by an interesting idea about the difficulty of political freedom. Walking in Vienna behind the monument of Gutenberg, thinking hopefully of peace and democracy, I was suddenly struck by the thought that democracy can never become really stabilized. For just when freedom gets stabilized, people will begin to take it for granted; and if they do, freedom will be in danger. They won't cherish it any longer because they will not be able to imagine what the loss of freedom might mean: perhaps terrorism, and perhaps war.

In spite of experiencing this flash of insight, I became attracted to the Communist Party when it claimed to be the party of peace, at the time of the Treaty of Brest-Litovsk in March 1918. There was much talk of peace in those days before the end of the First World War, but nobody except the Communists was willing to make political sacrifices for it: this was Trotsky's claim at Brest-Litovsk, and his message to the rest of the world. I certainly got the message, although I did not trust the Bolsheviks. I had heard much from a Russian friend about their fanaticism and their habit of lying. But their new declaration of pacifism attracted me.

After the collapse of the German and Austrian empires, I decided for various reasons to leave school and educate myself for the university entrance examinations. Not long after this, I decided in a tentative spirit to try out what the Communist Party was like. It must have been approximately in April 1919 that I went to Party Headquarters and offered myself as a voluntary errand boy. By then I knew quite a bit about Marxist theory; and although I was too young for party membership I was welcomed with open arms by the top party bosses themselves, who made use of me for all sorts of services. I was, strangely enough, often present at their less secret conferences, and I learnt an immense amount about their ways of thinking. I had a very close escape from falling into the Marxist *ideological mousetrap* (as I called it much later). I was strongly motivated by what I felt to be my moral duty; and it was this that almost caught me.

I shall now describe the ideology and the trap, and then, as my next point, how I escaped from it through the moral shock of a terrible experience, and through a great moral revulsion.

Marxist theory, or Marxist ideology, has several aspects, but the most important by far is that *it is a theory of history*, supposedly capable of predicting the future of mankind with absolute scientific certainty (though only in broad outline). More especially, it claims that it can predict social revolution, just as Newtonian astronomy can predict eclipses of the sun and the moon. The fundamental idea on which Marx based his theory is this: *All history is the history of class struggle.*

Marx first announced in 1847, at the end of his book *The Poverty of Philosophy*, that the class struggle must lead to a social revolution that would establish a classless or communist society. His argument was very brief. Since the working class (or 'the proletariat') is the one and only oppressed class left, and since it is also the only producing class, as well as the class to which the vast majority belong, it must necessarily win. But its revolutionary victory must lead to the elimination of all other classes, and thereby to a society in which only *one* class is left. But a one-class society is a classless society – a society in which there is neither a dominant nor a repressed class. It therefore is a communist society, as Marx and Engels declared a year later in their *Communist Manifesto*.

Since all history is the history of class struggle, the classless society will be the end of history. There will be no more wars, no more struggles, no more violence, no more repression; state power will wither away. Or, in religious terminology, there will be heaven on earth.

By contrast, the existing society, which Marx called 'capitalism', was, in his eyes, a society in which the capitalists had total domination – in fact, a class dictatorship. Marx showed in his colossal work *Capital* – three volumes totalling 1,748 pages – that the number of capitalists must, owing to the *law of the concentration of capital*, become fewer and fewer, while that of the workers will increase. And by a similar law, the *law of increasing misery*, the workers will be more and more impoverished, while the capitalists will grow richer and richer. The intolerable misery of the workers will turn them into radical revolutionaries, conscious of their revolutionary class interests. The workers of all countries will unite and carry out the social revolution. Capitalism with its capitalists will be destroyed – *liquidated*; and there will be peace on earth.

Today, the history predicted by Marx is no longer credible; and Western Marxists no longer hold these views – although they still propagate the theory that we live in a beastly and morally rotten 'capitalist' world. But Marxism was still credible in the hungry years of the First World War and the still hungrier time following it; and it was still accepted by outstanding physicists and biologists very much later. Einstein was no Marxist, aware that theories, including his own, are usually far from satisfactory. But he was certainly a sympathizer and even an admirer of Marxism. Several leading British scientists, among them J.B.S. Haldane and J.D. Bernal, were Party members. They were actually attracted by the claim of Marxist theory to have the status of a historical science. Bernal said not long before Stalin's death that Stalin was the greatest living scientist, and one of the greatest scientists ever. To show you the seriousness of this claim to scientific status: there is a book written by Alexander Weissberg, a Viennese physicist now dead whom I knew well before he went to Russia in 1931 out of enthusiasm for Stalin. There he was imprisoned in 1936 during the great purge, tortured many times and kept in terrible conditions until the Hitler–Stalin Pact in 1939, when Stalin sold him and many other Communists from Germany and Austria to Hitler – certainly the meanest sale in history. He was put with all the others into Hitler's concentration camps; he escaped and was recaptured several times, and ultimately he was freed by Soviet troops in 1945. But in his very interesting book, in which he reports his experiences in Stalin's prisons, we get a hint at the end that he still believes in Marx's theory of history. I met him in 1946 in London, and when he first told me about his experiences, I thought he was cured. Not so. When his book came out in Germany in 1951, and when I saw him again some years later, he still believed in the Marxist theory of history, although he admitted that it is in need of several corrections. Of course, I tried hard to convert him, but I am doubtful whether I succeeded where Stalin's prisons had failed.

I want to mention three further believers and great scientists. First, there were the Joliot-Curies, the two famous physicists: Irene, daughter of Madame Curie the discoverer of radium, and Irene's husband, Frédéric. In 1935 they jointly received the Nobel Prize for Chemistry; both were members of the Resistance and the French Commission for Atomic Energy; but both were active members of the French Communist Party until their death.

Then there is Andrei Sakharov, father of the Russian nuclear fusion bomb. I was, and still am, a great admirer of Sakharov the dissenter:

I made a public speech in support of him in New York on his sixtieth birthday, appealing to the Soviet government to free him. But from his *Memoirs* I learned to my surprise how deeply he believed, at the age of forty, in the official Communist doctrine. When Stalin died, Sakharov shed tears over the death of a great humanitarian, as he tells us; and at least until 1961, when he was forty, he believed in the theory of the necessary Revolution and its necessary cruelties, committed by that great humanitarian. Later in life he changed his mind radically.

Now, by the 'Marxist trap' I do not mean only the allegedly scientific theory that leads to Marxist historical prophecy. I mean, rather, the moral chains by which a believer in this prophecy may find himself bound to the Party. I have a vivid memory of these moral chains that, together with the belief in the prophecy, constitute the trap.

I was from the beginning somewhat sceptical about the paradise resulting from the revolution. I certainly disliked the existing society in Austria, in which there were hunger, poverty, unemployment, and runaway inflation – and currency speculators who managed to profit from it. But I felt worried about the Party's obvious intention to arouse in its followers what seemed to me murderous instincts against the 'class enemy'. I was told that this was necessary, and in any case not meant quite so seriously; and that in a revolution only victory was important, since more workers were killed every day under capitalism than would be killed during the whole revolution. I grudgingly accepted that, but I felt I was paying heavily in terms of moral decency. And then there were the lies told by the leaders. Clearly, they were saying one thing one day and quite the opposite the next; and the day after something quite different again. For example, they would deny the Red Terror one day and assert its necessity the next. Mistakes might occur, but they must never be questioned since loyalty to the Party line had to be absolute. Only Party discipline could hasten victory. And while I again grudgingly accepted this, I felt that I was having to sacrifice for the Party something like my personal honesty.

But then came the catastrophe. One day in June 1919 a Party-sponsored demonstration of unarmed young comrades was fired upon by the police, and there were a number of deaths (eight if I remember rightly). I was outraged at what the police had done, but also at myself. For not only had I taken part; I had approved of the Party's sponsorship and, perhaps, encouraged others to join in. Possibly some of them were among the dead. For what had they died? I felt responsible for them. I decided that although I had a right to risk my own life for the sake of my ideals, I certainly had no right to encourage others to risk their life for my ideals – and even less for a theory like Marxism of whose truth there *might* be some doubt.

I asked myself whether I had seriously and critically examined the Marxist theory. And I was deeply depressed when I had to admit to myself that the answer was: 'No'.

But when I returned to Party headquarters I found a very different attitude: the revolution demanded such sacrifices; they were unavoidable. And it meant progress, for it would make the workers furious with the police, and conscious of the class enemy.

I never went there again. I had escaped from the Marxist trap.

But now I embarked upon a very critical study of Marxism.

For various reasons – mainly because I did not wish to encourage fascism – I published the results only twenty-six years later, in my book *The Open Society and Its Enemies*. Meanwhile, I had published some other results: I had developed a criterion to decide whether or not a theory deserved the status of a science – a science such as Newtonian astronomy, for example.

I cannot, in this lecture, discuss the many points on which Marx's theory of history is wrong. In my book on the open society I have given a detailed analysis and critique of the Marxist prophecy. Here I wish only to point out what is most obvious: that 'capitalism' in Marx's sense no longer exists. The society that Marx knew has undergone great, indeed wonderful, revolutions. The once intolerably heavy and exhausting manual work that millions of men and women had to do has disappeared from our Western societies. I still witnessed it; and nobody who has not known it himself can have any idea of the difference – a revolution indeed, which we owe to the much-maligned growth of technology.

Altogether, the opposite of what Marx predicted has happened. The workers have become less wretched, and many are happy in the Western democracies. Of course, the Left's propaganda – both red and green – still spreads belief in the beastliness of our world and in our unhappiness. In this way, most unfortunately, it even spreads unhappiness itself, for happiness is partly dependent upon what we think. But speaking as a historian, I maintain that our open society is the best and most just that has so far existed on earth.

Obviously, there no longer exists the society that Marx once called 'capitalism'; and there is no reason why we should continue to mislead ourselves by calling our society by that name.

But I can say more. 'Capitalism' in the historical sense used by Marx has *never* existed on this earth; there has never existed a society with an inbuilt tendency like Marx's 'law of increasing misery', or a hidden dictatorship of the capitalists. All this was and is sheer delusion. Admittedly, the early days of industrialization were terribly hard. But industrialization also meant increased productivity and it soon meant mass production. Obviously, some of the mass production sooner or later found its way to the masses. Marx's historical picture with its prophecy is not only false; it is impossible. You cannot mass-produce for a small, dwindling number of rich capitalists.

So indeed: Marx's capitalism is an impossible mental construct, a delusion.

But in order to destroy what was a delusion, the Soviet Union amassed the greatest arsenal the world has ever seen, including masses of nuclear weapons. Expressed in units of Hiroshima bombs, they are equivalent to tens of millions; perhaps even more. All to destroy a delusion of hell, for its alleged beastliness. The reality was, to be sure, not heaven – but it was far nearer than the Communist reality was to heaven.

So, I have come a second time to the same conclusion – from a different side, from the logical analysis and criticism of Marxist ideology.

We must never again allow such ideologies to take hold of us.

I now turn to the final part of my lecture. What can we learn from the past for the future? And what can we recommend to our politicians?

First, we must break with the ridiculous habit of thinking that a wise man can predict what *will* happen. It seems that almost everybody believes it is characteristic of wisdom to make true prophecies. And almost everybody believes that a rational programme for the future must be based upon a true prediction.

And everybody looks at human history as a mighty river that rolls along before our eyes. We can see it as it comes down from the past; and if our view is well informed, we must be able to predict at least the general direction of its future course.

For many people this sounds all right, apparently. But it is all wrong – even morally wrong. It ought to be replaced by a very different way of seeing history. I propose the following.

History stops today. We can learn from it; but the future is never a prolongation of the past; nor is it an extrapolation. The future does not exist yet. Our great responsibility lies precisely in the fact that we can influence the future, that we can do our best to make it better.

To do this we must use all we have learnt from the past; and one very important thing we ought to have learnt is: *to be modest.*

So what do I propose to do?

We have seen that the past was bedevilled by a Left–Right polarization largely resulting from a belief in a non-existent capitalist hell that had to be destroyed for humanity's sake, even if humanity went under in the process. It almost did; but now we can hope that this insane delusion will no longer be influential (though I fear it will take a long time to wither away completely).

I propose that we make a great effort to disarm not only externally, in our foreign relations, but internally: that is, we should try to conduct politics without a Left–Right polarization.

I believe that this is difficult to achieve. I am sure that it is possible.

But have there not always been Left parties and Right parties? Perhaps; but there was never, before Lenin, this mad polarization, this hate and fanaticism, backed by this 'scientific' certainty. Winston Churchill could move in Parliament from one side to the other. It caused scandal and outrage, even some lasting personal bitterness, perhaps a feeling of betrayal. But all this was on another level from that of the present Left–Right polarization – even though good Communists always lived in danger of an accusation of betraying the Party and, if they happened to be in the Soviet Union, of imprisonment or liquidation. The difference may perhaps be described as follows.

To normal people, such things as spying, and, worst of all, spying among friends, are still an unspeakably horrible and inconceivable activity. But it was this that many a good Communist was accused of, at least in Stalin's time – if, that is, a formal accusation of any kind was made. This shows the kind of atmosphere that the Left–Right polarization created in its extreme forms. It is certainly possible to get rid of this in an open society.

What should we put in place of the Left–Right polarization? Or, perhaps better: what programme can we set against the Left–Right polarization, with the hope of superseding it?

I propose that one of the parties – I hope one of the major parties – declares:

We can now dismantle the ideological war machines, and we can all adopt a more or less common humanitarian programme such as the following. (Note that even if our programmes should fully agree, there should be at least two parties, so that the opposition can control the honesty and the administrative skill of the majority party.) Our tentative programme is this, and we are keen to discuss and improve it.

1. *Strengthening Freedom, Controlled by Responsibility.* We hope to achieve something like a maximum degree of personal freedom, but this is possible only in a civilized society – that is, a society devoted to a life of non-violence. Indeed, this is the distinguishing characteristic of a civilized society: that it constantly searches for peaceful, non-violent solutions to its problems.

2. *World Peace.* Now that the atom bomb and nuclear warheads have been invented, all civilized societies ought to cooperate in keeping the peace and closely monitoring the proliferation of atomic and hydrogen weapons. This is indeed our first duty, for otherwise civilization will disappear and, shortly after it, humanity itself. (This simple truth will be described as Western ideological imperialism – an accusation that is very clever, but totally irrelevant.)

3. *Fighting Poverty.* Thanks to technology, the world is wealthy enough, at least potentially, to eliminate poverty and also to reduce unemployment to a tolerable minimum. Economists have found this very difficult – as no doubt it is; and they have ceased, rather suddenly (about 1965), to regard it as their main aim, as it was before. It seems a problem that has suddenly become unfashionable, and many economists behave as if there were a proof that it was insoluble. But on the contrary, there exists more than one proof that the problem is soluble, even though it may be very difficult to avoid some interference with the free market. But we interfere constantly with the free market, probably much more than necessary. The solution to this problem is urgent, and its being out of fashion is scandalous. If economists cannot come up with better methods, we must simply use necessary public works, especially privatized public works such as road-building, school-building, teacher-training, etc., and intensify them in periods of increasing unemployment for the purpose of a counter-cyclical policy.

4. *Fight the Population Explosion.* With the invention of abortion pills, in addition to other methods of birth control, biochemical technology has achieved a state where education on population control should be made available all over the world. The doctrine that this would be a Western imperialist policy can be countered if the open societies work to reduce further their own (already declining) populations.

This point is of the greatest urgency, and should be high on the political agenda of all parties with a humanitarian programme. For all our so-called environmental problems are essentially due to the population explosion, as a moment's thought should suffice to convince everybody. For example, it may be true that our expenditure of energy per person is increasing, and ought to be reduced. But if this is so, it is still so much more urgent to attack the causes of the population explosion, which appear to be connected to poverty and illiteracy. For humane reasons, besides, we must work towards the goal that only children who are wanted are born, since it is cruel to produce an unwanted child, and this too often leads to violence, both mental and physical.

5. *Education to Non-Violence.* It is my considered opinion (though, of course, I may be wrong) that violence has lately been on the increase. At any rate, this is a hypothesis that can be investigated. And it should also be investigated whether we are educating our children to a toleration of violence. If we are, then action is urgently needed; for an attitude of acceptance of violence would clearly threaten our civilization. But altogether, do we watch properly over our children, ready with the care they may need? This is a point of the greatest importance, for obviously our children are, from an early age, almost completely in our hands, and our responsibility for them is immeasurable.

It is clear that this is closely connected with some of the previous points, such as the population explosion. I believe we should try to teach our children, if not the virtue of non-violence at least the truth that the greatest vice of all, the greatest of all evils, is cruelty. I do not say 'unnecessary cruelty', for cruelty is not only never necessary, it is never permissible. This includes mental cruelty, which we often commit out of thoughtlessness, that is, stupidity, laziness, or selfishness.

It has become unfashionable, I fear, to speak of these educational problems, both because of the fashionable freedom to do as one pleases (even if it is vicious according to unfashionable morals) and because, I admit, there is so much hypocrisy connected with morality. To this I say: Kant told us, 'Dare to be wise!' I may perhaps, more modestly, tell you: Dare to despise fashions, and be a little more responsible each day. This is, perhaps, the best you can do for freedom.

13

THE NECESSITY OF PEACE*

I thank you all, and especially the committee of the German Society for the United Nations, for the great honour I have been given today. That this honour is associated with the name of Otto Hahn has moved me most deeply.

Twenty years before he discovered the splitting of uranium, Otto Hahn was already one of my heroes – one of those great researchers in the fields of radiochemistry and atomic theory who discovered new radioactive elements, new atoms, and new forms of radiation. But they also invented new theories, important new hypothetical natural laws to describe and explain certain physical relationships between different forms of radiation, between the transformations of radioactive atoms.

Already in 1918, when I was sixteen years old, Otto Hahn figured as one of the real Greats, alongside Pierre and Marie Curie, Ernest Rutherford, William Ramsay, and the theorists Max Planck, Albert Einstein, and Niels Bohr. It was at the Physics Institute on Boltzmangasse in Vienna that I first heard of these great scientists, nuclear physicists and radiochemists, from my now long-dead friend Franz Urbach, who was working under Stefan Meyer at the Vienna Institute for Radio Research. A few years later, I read more about Otto Hahn in a textbook entitled *Atomic Theory* (first edition 1924) written by my teacher Arthur Haas, an important though today almost forgotten atomic scientist. I have looked up my well-thumbed copy of the second edition, dated 1929, and my memory was not wrong. On page 183 there is a sentence reporting both the discovery of radium

* Speech in acceptance of the Otto Hahn Peace Medal, on 17 December 1993 in Berlin.

and polonium by the Curies, and the discovery of protactinium by Otto Hahn and Lise Meitner.

So the name of Otto Hahn is associated with my earliest memories from the heroic age of the great atomic discoveries. I also have personal memories from the interwar period of Ernest Rutherford, Niels Bohr, Otto Robert Frisch, and Lise Meitner. But I never met Otto Hahn.

After the end of the Second World War, Frisch told me of Hahn's despair on hearing of the destruction of Hiroshima. At first Hahn felt jointly responsible when this terrible news reached him and the other German atomic scientists then interned in England. He was most deeply affected. Later Frisch also told me of Hahn's educational work on atomic weapons – his arguments against the atomic arming of Germany and for the absolute necessity of peace.

Ever since my early youth, I have admired Otto Hahn as a scientist and a human being. And after admiring him for seventy-five years, I am now given this great honour associated with his name: the Otto Hahn Peace Medal. But it is not only the name of Otto Hahn that means so much to me. All through my life, and especially since the outbreak of the First World War – on a day I still remember very well – the problem of securing peace has accompanied me as a personal responsibility.

I ask all of you associated with the bestowing of the Peace Medal to accept my thanks. I should like to thank also everyone who has come here to show their commitment to the absolute necessity of peace and to the necessity of strengthening the United Nations.

I have already spoken of the pantheon of scientists, especially nuclear physicists and radiochemists such as Otto Hahn, of whom I first heard in 1918 at the Physics Institute in Vienna. But long before that, something had happened that had laid the basis of my admiration for those scientists, and that later also contributed to my enthusiasm for the League of Nations, the predecessor of the United Nations. At Christmas 1908 my elder sister Dora received a book that interested me enormously, and a book that, because she did not share my burning interest, she gave me as a present a year later. It was a book by the Norwegian explorer Fridtjof Nansen, who helped in the founding of the League of Nations after the First World War and remained one of its most important and active figures up to his death in 1930. The book that so captivated me as a seven-year-old was the German edition of his *Farthest North*, a record of the Norwegian polar expedition that lasted more than three years between 1893 and 1896. It began, then, a hundred years ago on the ship *Fram*, which Nansen had had built in such a way that it would be lifted by the ice-floe instead of being crushed by it. For nearly thirty-five months the ship was enclosed by polar ice, yet in accordance with Nansen's plans it rode across the Arctic basin from the New Siberian Islands to Spitzbergen.

No other book had such an influence on my childhood. It aroused my interest in discoveries – not only voyages of discovery, but also theoretical discoveries. It was Nansen's book that revealed to me as a child the importance of bold theories, of daring, even too daring, hypotheses. For the planning of Nansen's expedition was based upon theoretical considerations and bold ideas. He reports that his ideas were sharply criticized, especially by expert predecessors in polar research. These experts attacked Nansen's brilliant plans as fantastic and suicidal, predicting that the *Fram* would, like previous ships, be crushed by the ice. But Nansen put up an astute defence. His voyage through three long Arctic winters became an experimental test of his daring but well thought-out theories.

The idea that research, including scientific and theoretical research, consists of advancing bold hypotheses and testing them experiment-ally was thus already clear to me as a child. It is to Nansen that I owe this perhaps somewhat romantic view of science as consisting of experimental investigations and *not* of results assured for all time. True science, then, primarily consists of discoveries that have to be repeated over and over again – it does *not* consist of so-called solid facts but of unsure *hypotheses*. The researcher must therefore sometimes take risks that put his intellectual responsibility severely to the test.

Charles Darwin already stressed that one cannot experiment with-out hypotheses. But Nansen went still further. He said that even quite wild hypotheses are better than none at all, and he gave as examples the three ancient Nordic legends or sagas, the three hypotheses of an ice-free route for ships to Japan and China: (1) the North-East Passage, in northern Asia; (2) the North-West Passage in the north of North America; and (3) an ice-free polar basin opening the way directly via the North Pole. Of these three theories, Nansen writes in the introduction to his book: 'Wild as these theories were, they have worked for the benefit of mankind; for by their means our knowledge of the earth has been widely extended . . . [N]o work done in the service of investigation is ever lost, not even when carried out under false assumptions.'[1]

When I read this book over and over again in my childhood, I had no idea how lasting its influence on me would be. Only now do I see it, with astonishment. And now it is also clear to me that I owe to

Nansen's influence my interest in atomic physics – and my reverence for nuclear physicists and radiochemists such as Otto Hahn.

A few months ago, when I had already decided to write about my two heroes Hahn and Nansen in this speech of thanks, I was completely unaware that they had been friends. Last month Dietrich Hahn, Otto's grandson, sent me a book about his grandfather originally written by Walter Gerlach, which now contains some important further material by Dietrich himself. Quite by chance, my assistant opened the book at page 142 and read this to me: 'A lively correspondence about geological matters subsequently developed between Hahn and Fridtjof Nansen. Among other things, Hahn confirmed Wegener's theory of continental drift.'

You cannot imagine my astonishment! I had known nothing of this when I was writing my speech and told of my two heroes, Otto Hahn and Fridtjof Nansen, who both worked for science and for peace.

The reference to Alfred Wegener in the quotation from Dietrich Hahn's book was also of the greatest interest to me, for Wegener was another scientist-hero from my childhood who, like Nansen, risked his life to test his theories. He died in 1930 (the same year as Nansen) at the age of fifty, on his third Greenland expedition to the centre of the glaciated high plateau.

There are two reasons why I wanted to mention Nansen in this talk: first, because he aroused my interest in scientific research; and second, because he did so much for peace after 1918 as High Commissioner of the International Red Cross and the League of Nations. One of his greatest deeds is not yet totally forgotten. After the First World War he created the Nansen passport, which was introduced in 1922. This travel document for stateless refugees was gradually recognized by a total of fifty-two countries – first for refugees from Russia, but soon from anywhere in the world.

Nansen's other action, now almost forgotten, was the aid to a starving Soviet Union that he largely organized through the League of Nations in Geneva. It was the first international aid of its kind, lasting from 1921 to 1923. Only with great difficulty did Nansen obtain Lenin's permission to send and distribute through his international organization food and medicine to the sick and starving. What Lenin mainly feared, I suppose, was espionage and revelations about the terrible conditions in the Soviet Union. In 1923, after the operation was over, Lenin himself said that Nansen Aid had saved the lives of three million people. Other reports (which I am unable to check) spoke of seven million.

I found to my regret that this important operation (which set an example for the United Nations) was soon forgotten; and this is why I have mentioned it. Whenever during the Cold War I met someone (especially an active diplomat) who I thought should know something about Nansen Aid to the Soviet Union, I asked him about it. But none had ever heard of it. It seems right to recall that episode in the pre-history of the United Nations. It is immeasurably important for us to learn from history, and also important to learn from the distorting and forgetting of history. I suspect that Nansen Aid was so soon forgotten because both the Soviets and Left intellectuals in the West found it uncomfortable to recall it.

I do not know the letters that Hahn and Nansen wrote to each other after the First World War. But although their theme was geophysics, they presumably contained something about Nansen's activity for peace. Nansen died in 1930. Did Hahn remember him after 1945, after the Second World War, when he began his work for peace and against atomic weapons? I suspect not. The reason for Hahn's peace work was simply that, knowing more than other citizens about atomic weapons, he felt it his duty to speak about this issue that was so crucial for mankind. He could makes things clear; he had to use his knowledge.

Use his knowledge for what? For an age-old wish of humanity. *Et in terra pax* – peace on earth. This is what we read in the New Testament. It is what we hear and are shaken by at one point in Beethoven's *Missa Solemnis*. It is how the League of Nations was created after the First World War – the league originally called for by Immanuel Kant, the greatest of all modern philosophers, in his book *On Perpetual Peace* (1795). It is how the United Nations was founded after the Second World War, with the great hope of establishing world peace. And it is why Otto Hahn, with atomic weapons in mind, wrote shortly before his death of the 'necessity of world peace'.

Peace is necessary. Perhaps it will have to be fought for and defended for a long time to come. We must be prepared for that. And also be prepared for ourselves and the United Nations to make mistakes. But optimism is a duty.

Before I finish, I should just like to clarify this phrase, 'Optimism is a duty'.

The future is open. It is not fixed in advance. So no one can predict it – except by chance. The possibilities lying within the future, both good and bad, are boundless. When I say, 'Optimism is a duty', this means not only that the future is open but that we all help to decide it through what we do. We are all jointly responsible for what is to come.

So we all have a duty, instead of predicting something bad, to support the things that may lead to a better future.

Note

1   *Farthest North,* Constable & Co., London, 1897, p. 7.

14

MASARYK AND
THE OPEN SOCIETY*

To be in Prague again after sixty years (and they have been difficult years for everybody): this is a great experience. I visited Prague from Vienna in 1912 and 1913, before the First World War, and also several times during the war. And it was at the latest in 1934 that I decided Prague was the most beautiful city in Central Europe. This has not changed. But everything else has.

Sixty years ago Tomás Garrigue Masaryk, the great founder of the Republic of Czechoslovakia and its liberator-president, was residing in the Hradschin Castle. I deeply admire Masaryk. He was one of the most important pioneers of what I called, a year or two after his death, the open society. He was a pioneer of an open society, both in theory and in practice – indeed, the greatest of its pioneers between Abraham Lincoln and Winston Churchill.

Of the successor states of the Austrian Empire, now defeated and impoverished, Masaryk's creation was the only successful one. Czechoslovakia was a financial success, an industrial success, a political success, an educational success, and a cultural success; and it was well defended.

Never was a new state – after all, the result of a revolution – so peaceful and so successful, and so much the creative achievement of one man. And all this was not due to a lack of great difficulties; it was the result of Masaryk's philosophy, his wisdom, and his personality, in which personal courage, truthfulness, and openness played so conspicuous a role. This is indeed what it was. But humanism, or humanitarianism, also played a dominant role.

* Lecture given at the Charles University, Prague on 25 May 1994 on the occasion of being awarded an honorary doctorate.

Masaryk's extraordinary life has, I expect, been closely studied by historians. Nevertheless, I have come to Prague in possession of two stories, or anecdotes, that are very probably quite unknown to all his biographers. I think both stories may, at least in part, still be testable by someone interested in researching the documents that may still be extant.

The first is the story of the strange circumstances under which I first heard Masaryk's name mentioned, in the winter of 1915-16 during the First World War, when I was thirteen years old.

My father was a lawyer in Vienna, and a family by the name of Schmidt, with their three sons and a daughter, were close friends of our family. One son was a professional army officer; another, Dr Karl Schmidt, then in his late twenties, was a lawyer; and the third, Oscar, was a pupil in my class at school. Dr Karl Schmidt frequently came to see us, and he often stayed for dinner. On one of these evenings, dressed in his wartime uniform of an officer in the Austrian Imperial Army, he told us that his current duty was to investigate cases of high treason and to prepare court-martial proceedings against the traitors. He told us of a most interesting case he was then pursuing: the case of a 66-year-old professor of philosophy at the University of Vienna, Dr Tomâŝ Masaryk, who was currently living in England or the United States, one of the main leaders of the Czech and Slovak Movement for National Independence and, most obviously, a man guilty of high treason – but, Schmidt continued in strictest confidence, a wonderful man.

Schmidt told us he was reading Masaryk's books, especially one about Russia's relations with Europe, which he found most impressive. Warming to his subject, Schmidt gave us a lecture on this incredible traitor, a man of the highest learning and culture, a leading philosopher, a teacher of ethics, a great liberal, and a man prepared to risk his life to achieve the freedom of what he regarded as his people. Later Schmidt also told us of the army that Masaryk was organizing abroad against Austria and Germany, from Czechs living in France, Britain, the Soviet Union, and the United States, and also from Austrian Czech soldiers who had become prisoners-of-war in Russia.

This was an extraordinary experience, and it is vividly before me after seventy-eight years. It could have happened, I now think, only in Austria. Imperial Austria was then at war: special legislation made parliamentary control impossible, and its prime minister, Count Stürgkh, exercised dictatorial powers. And yet, the liberal atmosphere of the pre-war period was still alive in Vienna. Here was a lawyer, at the same time an army officer appointed to pursue treason – and he was obviously committing treason himself by telling us ordinary civilians, in confidence on each of his occasional visits, about the progress of his investigations and his admiration for a traitor! Yet clearly, he had no fear at all. He knew he was safe – in spite of the dictatorship and the state of martial law. What a difference from the situation that started a year later in Russia and led to that horrible thing we now call 'modern dictatorship'!

This was in 1916, in Vienna. But in some regions where the authorities faced irredentist nationalism, state terror ruled. The bureaucrats, the pocket dictators, were unaffected by the liberalism of the cities – and they were afraid. They ruled by secret terror, even torture: and I learned it all from the same extraordinary source, the recurrent visitor Dr Karl Schmidt.

Schmidt told us all about the movements of Masaryk, his hero against whom he was preparing a case that would be bound to lead to his execution if a victorious Imperial Austria ever got its hands on him. But by 1916 it had become clear even to me that this would never happen: that the Central Powers had lost the war.... What I did not know was that even some members of the Government of Austria wanted to give in, and that Austria continued with the war largely for fear of a German invasion.

This is the end of my first story.

Almost twenty years later, when Chancellor Schuschnigg was dictator of Austria, I again happened to hear something very personal about Tomáš Masaryk. At the University of Vienna I had been a pupil of Professor Heinrich Gomperz, the Greek scholar, and we had become friends. After the murder of Chancellor Dollfuss by a troop of Austrian National Socialists, Schuschnigg had taken over and demanded that all state and local government employees, including all teachers and professors, should join an organization he called the Patriotic Front, which admitted as members only people who signed a declaration that they were opposed to *Anschluss* with Germany (already under Hitler's dictatorship). All university professors signed (especially those who were Nazis). The one exception was Professor Heinrich Gomperz, whose family came from Germany and whose cultural background and Greek scholarship made him partial to a union with Germany where Greek scholars abounded. He himself was of Jewish descent and was well aware of Hitler's terroristic ethnic theories – and his terroristic practices. But he had faith in the high civilization of Germany and looked upon Hitler as a political freak, certain to disappear soon; he probably felt it beneath his dignity to take much account of Hitler. In most of this, Gomperz was sadly mistaken. However, his failure to sign up with Schuschnigg's Patriotic Front led to his dismissal and total loss of income; and the censorship prevented this from ever getting into the papers. Nobody heard of the dismissal. No rumour reached me, until one day he rang me and we met. Then he told me what had happened and said that he had decided to emigrate to the United States – except that he did not have money to pay for the costly journey. So he went to Prague, to ask his old colleague and friend Masaryk for a loan. Masaryk gave him the money from his own personal savings as a gift, rejecting a loan and explaining to Gomperz that he did not want to use any kind of official funds for the purpose because the political element might make it look pro-German or even pro-Hitler. And Gomperz told me how wonderful and how moving his meeting with Masaryk had been.

I have always admired Masaryk as one of the two great statesmen and heroes of twentieth-century Europe: I mean Masaryk and Churchill.

Masaryk's Czechoslovakia was, I do not doubt, the most open of all societies ever to develop in Europe. It lasted for only twenty years. But what difficult and what marvellous years! In the shortest time, this open society built a solid economy and the most solid military defence system in Europe. Then Masaryk's Czechoslovakia was destroyed by the two older European open societies – Britain and France, then governed by the appeasers. And we might speculate that, had Masaryk still been alive, it is improbable that they could have cooperated with Hitler in destroying Czechoslovakia. Hitler was still bluffing, and Masaryk, I believe, would have called the bluff.

But there was from the beginning an unnecessary weakness built into the structure of the Czechoslovakian open society. I am referring to the so-called 'principle of national self-determination', a principle that had acquired an almost absolute moral authority in the West (and it has not lost this authority even now) – although just a little thought should have told us all that this 'principle' is totally inapplicable in Europe, where even islands like Great Britain, Ireland, or Cyprus are populated by several so-called nationalities with political leaders claiming national self-determination. And Masaryk's open society was unable to give these claims a deeply considered moral and political response. It was only quite recently that your country again came under this pressure, and it had no well-thought-out theoretical and moral defence. And so it had to split. What the consequences will be, nobody knows.

No doubt, a homogeneous population that speaks one language has a tremendous advantage for the purpose of industrial collaboration. But where do you find this in Europe? Europe is just not like that, except in very few countries where it has been brought about by political and educational means, through the suppression of minorities and dialects. This holds especially for Germany and France. But even these two now have important minorities, and indeed all countries have. The exception left in Europe is Iceland (and possibly Malta).

I think that all lovers of peace and a civilized life should work to enlighten the world about the impracticability and inhumanity of that famous – or shall I say notorious? – 'principle of national self-determination', which has now degenerated into the ultimate horror of ethnic terrorism.

We must fight against such horrors. We must not fall prey to the cynical view that history is just violent and horrible, driven by the lust for gold and oil, for wealth and domination. This cynical interpretation of history is not true. European history begins with Solon's peaceful revolution that reformed the Constitution of Athens. By it, he freed those slaves who had been free citizens but had lost their freedom when unable to pay their creditors. Solon's revolution prevented this from ever occurring in Athens again. It was a long way from there to America and to Abraham Lincoln, who fell as the last of 600,000 white soldiers in a most terrible war that succeeded in freeing the negro slaves in the Southern Confederate States.

These are not just two exceptions in an otherwise endless history of greed and violence. Rather, they are two of the most important successes – admittedly, not very frequent successes – among the many defeats and setbacks we have suffered, often through our own mistakes, in our ceaseless struggle for freedom and justice.

And now, when we are again suffering setbacks, we must think of our very latest success: South Africa. And we must keep fresh in our memory such incredible achievements of the spirit of freedom, openness, and humanity as that of Churchill's seemingly hopeless resistance to Hitler after the fall of France, and Masaryk's return with his valiant army of 60,000 men, through Siberia and Vladivostok, across the Pacific Ocean and the American continent, to found a great republic, an open society, strong enough to rise again after many a violent death.

15

HOW I BECAME
A PHILOSOPHER
WITHOUT TRYING*

Dear President Inamori,
Esteemed Members of the Inamori Foundation,
Distinguished Guests,
Dear Ladies and Gentlemen,

May I begin by thanking all of you for coming here to listen to us, the
Laureates of the Kyoto Prizes for 1992? You have come here to join us
in celebrating what undoubtedly must be, for all three of us, one of
the greatest and happiest occasions of our lives.

I understand that each of us is expected to give two lectures, of
which today's lecture is the first. While the second lecture is supposed
to be of interest to the specialists in our respective fields of work,
today's lecture, as I understand it, should tell you something about
our lives and how it happened that we devoted our interests and our
ambitions to the special fields in which we did our main work.

Now I think that I should warn you from the very beginning that,
in my particular case, unfortunately, this pattern for today's lecture
does not fit at all. I am standing here before you as a philosopher; and
I am known as a philosopher in Great Britain, in Japan, and in other
countries. It is in the field of 'Philosophical Thought of the Twentieth
Century' that I have been awarded the great Kyoto Prize. But never,
during the long course of my life, did I think 'I want to become a
philosopher', or even 'I want to study philosophy'. Nor did I ever in
my life look at myself with satisfaction as a philosopher. If other

---

* Address given on 11 November 1992 at Kyoto on the occasion of being awarded
the Kyoto Prize together with Maurice Vincent Wilkes (in Advanced Technology)
and Yasutomi Nishizuka (in Basic Sciences).

people – including some professional philosophers – choose to classify me under this heading, and rank me as a philosopher, then this happens without my having either planned or intended it.

Of course, at a certain stage in my life I had to decide upon the profession I wanted to adopt; and, after some wavering, I decided that I wanted to become a schoolteacher. At first I thought that I wanted to be a teacher in primary schools; later I wanted to be a teacher in secondary schools – of mathematics, physics, chemistry, and biology. With this aim in mind I left school prematurely in 1918 when I was sixteen and became a so-called 'extraordinary' student at the University of Vienna in mathematics and physics. Three years later I became an 'ordinary' student, and another seven years after that, in 1928, I received both my doctorate in philosophy and my teacher's certificate in mathematics, physics, chemistry, and biology.

However, I wrote my doctoral thesis in the field of psychology, under Karl Bühler, who was famous as a child psychologist. There were two reasons for this: first, because I was interested in education, and therefore in psychology; and second, because I had some ideas of my own in this field – quite enough for a doctorate I thought. By contrast, I rated the fields of mathematics and of physics so highly that I thought I should never be able to have a really original idea of my own in these two marvellous and difficult fields. But I would have made these my fields of research had I dared to do so, and had I not looked upon myself as a future schoolteacher.

Perhaps I should mention at once that, some years later, I did have some original ideas in both these fields: within mathematics, it was mainly in the axiomatization of probability theory, and within a field called lattice theory; for example, I gave the first proof of the theorem that if you have a (meet) semi-lattice with a relative measure function defined on it, then it becomes distributive upon defining the join – a theorem of interest in probability theory, in lattice theory, and in quantum physics. And in physics, I had a number of original ideas in the field of quantum mechanics. This was then a new theory, invented by Werner Heisenberg just one year before I was awarded my doctorate. This invention of Heisenberg's was very important. But it seemed soon to be superseded by Erwin Schrödinger's invention of wave mechanics: this looked very different but led to (almost) equivalent results, and it was a more intuitive approach. I met both Heisenberg and Schrödinger in 1935, and I remained a friend of Schrödinger's until his death in 1961; and I am still a friend of his family.

Let me stop here for a moment. You will see that I worked in too many fields to gain the kind of specialized knowledge that a creative leader in any of these fields would need. But I had studied all these subjects intensely for many years without thinking for a moment that I might attain such a leadership position. I studied only because of the burning interest and excitement which these various subjects had aroused in me. And also because I hoped one day to infuse my pupils with this interest and excitement. But if I had contemplated a career as a discoverer, or as a research worker in any of these fields, or as a leader in the advancement of science, then, of course, my way of working in perhaps ten different fields would have been sheer madness. However, I had no such ambition; not, at least, until very much later – until the publication of my book, *The Logic of Scientific Discovery*, in German, towards the end of 1934.

Since I am speaking about the fragmentation and dissipation of my powers in so many fields, I ought to add to all this yet another confession. I come from a musical family. My grandparents on my mother's side had been co-founders of an organization in Vienna known as *Gesellschaft der Musikfreunde.* Around the middle of the nineteenth century, this organization was instrumental in the building of what remained for a long time the most famous of all the concert halls in the world, the *Musikvereinssaal* in Vienna, which was designed mainly with Beethoven's symphonies in mind. When I was sixteen I began to compose, taking Johann Sebastian Bach as my ideal. Most of these compositions are lost, but one, a fugue for organ, had its first public performance in July of this year in the Escorial Palace near Madrid, in Spain, about seventy years after it was written.

Now I must draw your attention once again to the fact that I am standing here as a philosopher, and that of all my studies I have not yet mentioned to you the study of philosophy.

I think that I asked my first philosophic question when I was seven or eight years old: I asked my father to explain to me the concept of infinity, and the infinity of space. I said that I found it impossible to conceive of infinity, and that I wanted an explanation. My father advised me to ask one of his two brothers, from whom I received indeed an excellent explanation of what is technically called potential or Aristotelian infinity, in contrast to actual or Cantorian infinity. It was an explanation that satisfied me almost completely. In later years, Cantorian infinity left me somewhat puzzled and has done so ever since.

There were many more philosophical problems to come. When I was ten, the problem 'what is life?' fascinated me, and I proposed to myself and to one of my school fellows that life is a process of oxidation like the flame of a candle – a solution first envisaged, as I found out later, by the early Greek philosopher Heraclitus of Ephesus. Philosophical problems were occupying me even before I started reading philosophical books, of which there were plenty in my father's library. The first such book I attempted to read, though quite unsuccessfully, was Kant's *Critique of Pure Reason*. I could not understand a word: I had no idea what problems it purported to deal with. But soon I learnt that there was another book in my father's library that explained Kant's *Critique*, a book by Schopenhauer, entitled *The World as Will and Representation* (or '*as Will and Idea*'), and this, if I remember correctly, was the first philosophical book (at least the first very large philosophical book) that I read and, indeed, studied.

I found Schopenhauer difficult, yet I managed to learn a lot from him; and I went on to read both Schopenhauer and Kant. Once I could read Kant, I liked him better than Schopenhauer; and Kant left me with many unsolved problems that troubled me for many years. But the idea of becoming a philosopher myself – either in the sense of concentrating my reading mainly on such books as those by Kant and Schopenhauer, or in the sense of making philosophy my profession and writing philosophic books myself – never occurred to me; and if it had occurred to me, I certainly should have rejected it. For although some philosophical *problems* interested me greatly, I did not think myself capable of solving any of them. A system of philosophy like Schopenhauer's appeared to me fascinating but also incredibly ambitious; and I did not believe that his metaphysical theories were true. Also, I wanted to do something useful, like teaching. Besides, I found problems in physics more attractive, and Darwinism more exciting and far more convincing. This explains why I never made up my mind to study philosophy, although I read many philosophical books. Apart from Immanuel Kant, I loved and admired best one group of Greek philosophers: the so-called pre-Socratic philosophers, especially Heraclitus, Xenophanes, and Parmenides. I also loved and admired Socrates, the Athenian citizen who was put to death by a jury of 500 of his Athenian fellow citizens. His defence speech, which his pupil Plato published under the title *The Apology of Socrates*, is the most beautiful philosophic work I know.

Because I felt that it would be useful for me as a schoolteacher if I were able to master a craft like cabinet-making, I decided to learn that too; and I actually obtained the official certificate of the Austrian state that I had become a qualified cabinet-maker.

It was while working at a cabinet-maker's bench that I arrived at what I may describe as my first conscious solution of a philosophical problem. The problem concerned the origin of our Western system of classical music – tonality, harmony, and counterpoint. I did not write it down, and I never talked about it to anyone; but fifty years later, in 1969, I described it briefly in a short chapter of an autobiographical book entitled *Unended Quest*, which was published some years later, in 1974. To my great surprise, I was told this year, in May 1992, that my very old theory of 1919 or 1920 of the origin of Western music was almost identical with a theory published at the same time by the famous German sociologist Max Weber.

I have told this story because it is, I am afraid, characteristic of my whole life. Neither my modest results in Greek scholarship (which led to new historical theories about Plato and the pre-Socratics) and in the sciences, nor those in philosophy (in epistemology and in the now so-called philosophy of science, or in social and political philosophy, such as in the theory of the origin of language and in the theory of democracy) were, as a rule, derived by that process which is usually described as 'research'. Instead it was a process that could perhaps be described as follows. First, I become acquainted with a subject, maybe superficially to start with, then more deeply because I am fascinated by some *problem.* Then – in some cases soon, in other cases after some years, perhaps even after some new problems in other fields have begun to interest me more – a problem or an idea may crystallize in my mind and lead to intense work; that means, I begin to think intensely about the problem, I try to clarify it, simplify it, often in the light of a new idea, and the problem may considerably change its character. A tentative solution may turn up; and upon further intense work, this solution may change considerably, in interaction with the changing problem.

Sometimes all of this happens only in my mind, and the proposed solution is never written down; or it is written down fifty years later, as in the one case I described earlier. At other times, I may write down notes at various stages of the process, or I may draw a diagram. Sometimes I reach my main result quickly, but I have never published any new result quickly. Quite often I do not publish my result at all, but only tell my friends or pupils about it. Or I send my result to a friend in a sequence of letters, for his criticism. And sometimes I forget my result for years – or, worst of all, for ever. You will, I hope, realize that I do not recommend this method of working. On the contrary, I wish to discourage all my listeners from adopting so hazardous a method.

Although this is not a method that I should advise anyone to imitate, I confess that I personally lived very happily with it all my life. But my late wife who worked with me and for me, and who helped me wonderfully in my work, suffered terribly from my working method. It is a method which cannot guarantee that hard work will yield results. I certainly have worked very hard and so did my wife. Take for example my two-volume work, *The Open Society and Its Enemies*. It has just been re-published in a new and improved German translation, in order to celebrate my ninetieth birthday, and so I had to look through it to revise the translation. The two volumes, with some new *Appendices*, amount now to just over 1,000 pages; and they contain so much material, and so many suggestions and arguments, that I am surprised that I was ever able to write them all down. But the fact is that I wrote the book twenty-two times, always trying to clarify and to simplify it, and my wife typed and re-typed the whole manuscript five times (on a decrepit old typewriter). It then took two years and three months before it was published in 1945. No, I cannot recommend my method.

At the time when my first book, *Logik der Forschung*, was published in 1934 (its English title is *The Logic of Scientific Discovery*) I was a schoolteacher. When I first wrote the book, the finished manuscript was more than twice as long as the version that was finally published in 1934, but the publisher had told me by exactly how much I should cut the book down. I had developed the fundamental idea for this book in the winter of 1919–20; that is, I had worked on the idea for fourteen to fifteen years, at first with not the slightest intention of publishing it.

In June and July 1919 I had become deeply critical of the theories of Karl Marx, and I had begun to study them thoroughly in order to come to a rational judgment as to whether they were true or false. I considered it my duty to undertake this important study. I was only seventeen, and of course I never expected that anyone would listen to my findings, or be interested in whatever I might have to say about this subject. I undertook the study merely to satisfy myself about the truth of a theory that I regarded as a grave danger for mankind. The outcome of these investigations was published in my book *The Open Society and Its Enemies* twenty-five years later. Although this book has been in print continuously since it was published in 1945, it played only a small part in undermining Marxism and the Soviet Empire; a far smaller part than the famous books of my late friend Friedrich von Hayek, for example his book *The Road to Serfdom*. Hayek died in March this year.

Very early in my critical studies of Marxism, during the winter of 1919–20, I had identified some problems which, many years later, led to the publication of *Logik der Forschung*, my first *published* book, in 1934. An English translation (*The Logic of Scientific Discovery*) did not appear until twenty-five years later. (*Die beiden Grundprobleme der Erkenntistheorie*, my first *completed* book, remained unpublished from 1933 until 1979; that is, for forty-six years.) *The Poverty of Historicism* was published next, by Friedrich von Hayek who then edited the journal *Economica*. He published it as a series of articles in 1944 and 1945, and it was published as a book only ten years later, first in an Italian translation, and later in English and then in many other languages; in Japan, three editions were published in 1961, and two more in 1965 and 1966. In the 1960s several other Japanese translations appeared, and in 1973 my book *The Open Society and Its Enemies* came out in a Japanese translation. I am not so well informed about subsequent publications in Japan. All these three books were the late results of some of my early work, begun in the winter of 1919–20; all of them can be described as books on the theory of knowledge, or epistemology, or philosophy of science (although the second and the third were books on the philosophy of history, and of historical science).

I shall now briefly explain how these books came to be.

As I mentioned before, I had started to study Marxism in a critical spirit – the spirit of finding out whether what Marxism asserted was true or false.

Marx, Engels, and Lenin insisted that the Marxist system was a *science:* that it had the status and the authority of natural science; a status similar to that of Newton's theory of gravity. Now this assertion was of great importance in those days, many years before the modern attacks on the status and authority of the natural sciences. In those days, the assertion that a theory had the status of science implied that it was true; and it meant even more: it meant that its truth could be *demonstrated*. In other words, science in those days had a tremendous prestige in the West – a prestige like nothing else. The claim that Marxism is a science – or perhaps we should say more clearly that Marxism is a scientific theory – was therefore of great importance. For it meant, in those days, that Marxism was true, and beyond all criticism except, perhaps, by experts in this field of science.

I decided, in the autumn of 1919, to investigate the claim that Marxism is a science independently from the claim whether or not it is true that socialism or communism is bound to come as the next historical epoch or world period (which I, by that time, had begun to disbelieve, since the Marxian arguments seemed to me highly questionable).

So I decided to work, first of all, on the following problem: Is it true or false that Marxism is a *science*, like Newton's gravitational theory (which I greatly admired)? This problem pleased me, for I looked upon myself as a future teacher of physics, and any physics teacher, I felt, ought to know what are the criteria that give physics, or chemistry, the status of a science – or better still, what makes *any* allegedly natural science a genuine science. Or, in very different words: Why do I respect astronomy but despise astrology? So I was very pleased to have been able to replace a problem about Marxism (which I disliked) with a more general problem that included physics (which I loved – especially Newton's cosmology).

It was this *problem* that made of me, in the course of time, a philosopher of science.

I was only seventeen, and although I was a member of the Mathematical Institute of the University of Vienna, I had no idea how to tackle a problem like this. So I began just by thinking about it, feeling sure that this must be an old problem, and that all the great professors at the University – at any rate all the physicists – must be familiar with it, and must know the solution. But in the mathematics seminars, utterly different problems were discussed and there was no opportunity to raise a problem such as mine. When I tried to mention it to some of my fellow students, they were (with one exception) not interested.

I first started with the following attempted characterization: an assertion or a statement belongs to science *if it can be proved*; or, what amounts to the same, if *it is a demonstrably true proposition.* However, I knew even before starting that this characterization must be unsatisfactory and must be replaced by something better. I knew that in geometry, for example, we have the famous axioms and postulates and definitions of Euclid. (In those days, postulates and axioms were rarely distinguished any longer.) These are characterized as being *not demonstrable*, although they clearly belong to geometry – which is very much a science! Moreover, the chosen axioms and postulates and definitions are the very foundations of geometry: from them, all propositions of geometry are derived, as theorems.

I soon found that, in order merely to clarify my problem and before even beginning to work on a solution, I had to distinguish between purely formal systems such as mathematics, and the so-called empirical or natural sciences such as physics, chemistry, biology, geology, and also geography.

So I tried to study, in the Mathematical Institute, what was there called 'axiomatics', that is, the general theory of axiomatic systems; of these the greatest expert was David Hilbert. When, ten years later, I had to write a mathematical thesis for my teacher's examination, I chose to write it on the subject of axiomatics.

I soon arrived at a serviceable distinction between a purely *formal system* (like logic or mathematics) on the one hand and, on the other, a theory whose purpose is to refer to reality – or, more clearly, *to describe or explain something real*, such as do Newton's or Einstein's theories of gravitation.

So I was first led to a comparison between pure mathematics and the theory of gravitation, and then between Newton's theory and Einstein's theory. I studied these theories intensely, and the claims made for them by different physicists. I conducted all these studies merely because of my burning interest in the problems, and without being in the least aware that here or there I was also breaking new ground.

At the time, I had no prospects whatsoever of obtaining a teaching position, not even in a primary school. I had been too young by one year to fight as a soldier in the Imperial Austrian Army in the First World War; and all the available positions for teachers were, quite properly, reserved for the soldiers who came back from the war, or from the prison camps.

But I obtained work – at first unpaid – in institutions for children, mostly for neglected children. Later, I was lucky enough to have the opportunity of giving private lessons on quite different subjects, varying from mathematics to psychology and philosophy, to all kinds of students at the University of Vienna. Among them were a few American students; and since in those days the U.S. dollar was strong and the Austrian currency was weak, this form of teaching was quite satisfactory for both parties. And I had excellent opportunities to learn how to teach (and also, how *not* to teach).

This kind of life was by no means exceptional in Vienna at that time. On the contrary, the economic situation made it not infrequent. When, in 1923, the City of Vienna announced that it would in future employ, even in its primary schools, only teachers who had passed successfully through its newly founded Pedagogic Institute, I and others like myself applied for permission to become members of this new Institute, which was affiliated to the University of Vienna.

In those days, students in Vienna had to finance themselves. But at least we did not have to pay any fees to the Institute; and we had a good prospect of getting a (badly paid) teaching job at the end.

I was a student at the Pedagogic Institute for two most interesting years. We were taught both at the newly founded Institute and at the University; and as some of my fellow students at the Institute found the going very hard, it so happened that I myself became, unofficially and unbeknown to the Director of the Institute, a teacher at the Institute – obviously, an unpaid teacher – giving courses to my fellow students. At times when officially the classrooms were empty, I began to give lectures and seminars to students who had difficulties in following some of the lectures at the University which they, as members of the Institute, were bound to attend. As we had lots of intermediate examinations (called 'Colloquia') to pass at the University, my courses became special preparations for these University examinations. Only one of our University teachers, the psychologist Professor Karl Bühler, knew about my teaching activities, since I had to ask his permission to use his laboratory for my classes. He later said in a letter to me that the group of students I had prepared was the best he had ever examined.

Among my unofficial courses at the Pedagogic Institute were courses in Latin for those who had not been taught Latin at their secondary schools. The University in those days demanded a modest proficiency in this language from all its students. This language teaching to individual adult students taught me much about human language; it was an experience essential for the views on language which much later became part of my (very sketchy) theory on the origin of human language, which even now is still unpublished.

After leaving the Pedagogic Institute it took me another five years before I was appointed, first, as a primary school teacher and, after another year, as a secondary school teacher. During this period I wrote many papers – they filled a whole wardrobe by 1930 – on subjects that today would be said to belong to the philosophy of science. None of these were ever submitted for publication.

In 1930, shortly before starting as a primary school teacher, I met Professor Herbert Feigl, originally from Austria, who was the same age as myself, and who was now Professor of Philosophy in the United States and a member of the so-called 'Vienna Circle' of philosophers. After listening to my theories for a night, he said that I should write them down in a book. So I stopped writing papers and started writing a book which led to the publication of my *Logik der Forschung* in the autumn of 1934.

This book contained a theory of scientific knowledge and its growth, a theory of probability which I later much improved, and a critical interpretation of quantum mechanics. (Of this several important points have since been rediscovered by others.) My book was an immediate success. Of course, this success was confined to the small circle of those who were, in spite of Hitler's dictatorship in Germany and his devastation of the German universities (not to mention the threat of war) still capable of thinking about such abstract problems as those discussed in my book.

In spite of all this, I received excellent reviews not only from the main European countries, but even from America, and very soon invitations to lecture from several Polish, English, and even German universities. At the same time I also received intimidating threats from some of the national-socialist teachers at the school at which I was then teaching, and also from my very powerful school inspector.

So I decided to accept the lecturing invitations from England, and to try to emigrate to England. The lectures in England were also a success, and in 1937 I obtained a university appointment in New Zealand. I took up my appointment as a lecturer in philosophy at Canterbury University College, then a part of the University of New Zealand. It is now the University of Canterbury.

I had evolved from a schoolteacher to a professional philosopher, teaching in a university, without having ever chosen philosophy as my subject of study – in fact, without ever having tried to become a philosopher.

So how did it happen? The answer is: Although *I* had never decided to study philosophy, the *problems* I had taken up as my own had forced me to study many things, philosophy among them. So I must say that I owe everything to my beloved problems. I really fell in love with my first problem: how to find a criterion of the empirical-scientific character of a theory. And after I obtained a solution, I fell in love with my various other problems, among them historical problems about ancient Greece – from Homer and Xenophanes and Parmenides and Plato to modern times: to Kant, Hegel and Marx, and to Khrushchev and Gorbachev.

I should certainly not encourage anyone to adopt my own ways of studying as an example to be followed; rather, I should warn them against it. But I can recommend every serious student, and especially every serious science student, to look out for a beautiful problem that he can really love, and to which he is prepared to dedicate his life. This attitude will make it easy for him to try again and again to find a solution, and to be critical of his own efforts which, in most cases, will frequently have to be redoubled before they can be successful. Even if they appear to be successful, they should be most seriously questioned by himself, for they will usually be open to improvement. Einstein somewhere tells us that throughout the period from 1905 to 1915 when he was trying to generalize his so-called theory of relativity (which thereby became a geometrical theory of gravitational forces), he rejected a hopeful idea for a solution every few minutes. The constant consciousness of our own fallibility, and constant self-criticism combined with unlimited devotion to our main problem and its many problem-children and other subsidiary problems – this is what I can recommend to you with full conviction, from the bottom of my heart.

I wish to end with this advice: However happy you may be with a solution, never think of it as final. There are great solutions, but a final solution does not exist. All our solutions are fallible.

This principle has often been mistaken for a form of relativism, but it is the very opposite of relativism. We seek for truth, and truth is absolute and objective, and so is falsity. But every solution to a problem opens the way to a still deeper problem.

May my advice be a signpost on your way to a creative and happy life!

Ladies and Gentlemen, I thank you for your attention and for your patience.

SUBJECT INDEX

162

NAME INDEX